TALKING ACROSS
THE DIVIDE

TALKING ACROSS

THE DIVIDE

How to Communicate with People
You Disagree With and
Maybe Even Change the World

JUSTIN LEE

A TarcherPerigee Book

An imprint of Penguin Random House LLC
375 Hudson Street
New York, New York 10014
penguinrandomhouse.com

TarcherPerigee with tp colophon is a registered trademark of Penguin Random House LLC.

Most TarcherPerigee books are available at special quantity discounts for bulk purchase for sales promotions, premiums, fund-raising, and educational needs. Special books or book excerpts also can be created to fit specific needs. For details, write: SpecialMarkets@penguinrandomhouse.com.

Library of Congress Cataloging-in-Publication Data

Names: Lee, Justin, 1977–   author.
Title: Talking across the divide : how to communicate with people you
    disagree with and maybe even change the world / Justin Lee.
Description: New York, NY : Tarcherperigee, [2018] | Includes bibliographical
    references. |
Identifiers: LCCN 2018005203 (print) | LCCN 2018020177 (ebook) |
    ISBN 9780143132707 () | ISBN 9780525504634
Subjects: LCSH: Interpersonal conflict. | Interpersonal communication. |
    Interpersonal relations.
Classification: LCC HM1121 (ebook) | LCC HM1121 .L44 2018 (print) | DDC
    302—dc23
LC record available at https://lccn.loc.gov/2018005203

Printed in the United States of America
10 9 8 7 6 5 4 3 2 1

Book design by Elke Sigal

To Anne Lee, who showed me how
to change the world.

And to all the unsung heroes who fight each day
for nuance and understanding.

Thank you.

CONTENTS

The First Barrier | Ego Protection

The Second Barrier | Team Loyalty

CONTENTS

The Third Barrier | Comfort

The Fourth Barrier | Misinformation

The Fifth Barrier | Worldview Protection

CHAPTER 1

Echo-Chamber World

Physically speaking, we can not separate. We can not remove our respective sections from each other nor build an impassable wall between them. A husband and wife may be divorced and go out of the presence and beyond the reach of each other, but the different parts of our country can not do this. They can not but remain face to face, and intercourse, either amicable or hostile, must continue between them.

—Abraham Lincoln, 1861[1]

We are a nation divided.

Turn on the TV or hop online, and it doesn't take long to see evidence of our polarized mentalities. We disagree on race and religion, on science and social issues—but we don't just disagree; we're baffled by each other's views, and we have no idea how to get through to one another. Partisan bickering has created a gridlocked government that struggles to get even widely supported things done. Important scientific research is being stalled by competing groups' agendas. Culture wars are fracturing our families and tearing our communities apart.

"It's like we live on different planets," my friend Ryan said to me the other day.

He was talking about a rift between him and members of his family. They'd been close at one time, he told me. But in recent years, they'd found themselves more and more often on opposite sides of cultural battles. They were bitterly divided by national politics, by matters of faith and morality, and by shifting cultural views on a variety of issues.

Ryan wanted to be able to sit down with his family and talk through their differences—to help them understand where he was coming from and to hopefully change their attitudes on the issues that mattered most to him. But every time he tried talking to them, he just wound up frustrated. Their views didn't make any sense to him, his didn't make any sense to them, and every conversation seemed to wind up in an argument. Their communication was breaking down somewhere, and the rift between them was widening into an uncrossable chasm. Ryan had eventually fallen into the habit of swallowing his emotions and trying to "make nice" at family events, but it was eating away at him. He couldn't help wondering what could have happened to cause the people he loved to be so stubborn and to see the world so differently.

And Ryan's far from alone. I've spent twenty years focusing on divisive issues in our society, and in that time, I've met thousands of people just like him—people whose families, churches, communities, and workplaces are being torn apart by controversy and conflict, each side baffled by the other, each pointing to different "facts" and making different assumptions. It is, as Ryan says, almost as if we live on different planets.

Competing ideas have always been part of the American way of life. Our political system is built on contests between differing ideas, and our Constitution reflects the hard-fought compromises of founders who did not see eye to eye on everything. But those compromises wouldn't have happened without communication across lines of disagreement, and our political marketplace of ideas begins to fall apart if we're hearing completely different versions of the truth from completely different sources. For this "American experiment" to function, we have to be able to talk to one another.

But our attempts to communicate are failing, and nowhere is this more obvious than in the current state of American politics. Since 1994, the Pew Research Center has studied America's political polarization, and in that time, the value divide between Republicans and Democrats has only grown larger. In 2017, Pew found the largest partisan divide in the history of their research— a value gap nearly 250 percent as large as it had been.[2] Meanwhile, hostility between the parties has skyrocketed.[3] Fewer of us are moderate than ever before, and as we drift toward the left or the right, most of us who identify as either Democrats or Republicans report that we have "just a few" or no close friends in the opposing party.[4]

Ultimately, though, our political troubles are only a symptom of the underlying disease. An us-vs.-them mentality is taking over our public and private lives. Increasingly, we take our disagree-

An us-vs.-them mentality is taking over our public and private lives.

ments *not* to the people we disagree with but to our own echo chambers—spaces where we can talk *about*, rather than *to*, the other side—where like-minded people echo our own beliefs right back to us. Our opponents, too, are stuck in their own echo chambers, having their beliefs reinforced by people on their side rather than being encouraged to consider what *we* have to say. That's a problem, because some of our biggest challenges as human beings require working together.

A Foot on Each Side of the Divide

My own interest in this problem began with the issues closest to me.

I grew up on a cultural battle line; I don't remember ever not being aware of the culture wars. I was raised in a conservative, evangelical Christian family, with a faith that has stayed with me my entire life. I learned from a young age that my church held certain views on a variety of controversial issues, and I quickly embraced those views as my own—including a staunch opposition to homosexuality. As a teenager, I tended to lecture my friends on these issues, earning me the nickname God Boy, a badge I wore with pride.

But puberty brought complications. I wasn't attracted to girls like my male friends were; I was attracted to guys. At eighteen, I finally had to admit to myself that I was gay, a realization that turned my evangelical life upside down and forced me to rethink a lot of what I thought I knew about gay people. As I struggled to make sense of all the new information, I increasingly felt trapped between two worlds. And in college, when I made some gay friends for the first time, it was easy to see how far apart these two worlds were. My gay friends didn't understand my evangelical friends and family, and my evangelical friends and family didn't understand my gay friends. It was, indeed, as if we lived on different planets.

I began speaking and writing about this faith-sexuality divide, and soon I was hearing views on the subject from frustrated people all across the spectrum. I started a nonprofit that worked successfully for sixteen years to bridge the divide and bring families back together that had been torn apart by their disagreements. My first book, *Torn: Rescuing the Gospel from the Gays-vs.-Christians Debate*, resulted in a flood of letters to me from parents, pastors, and others telling me that I had completely changed their opinion on the topic. There was an advantage, I realized, to being caught between worlds: It made me culturally bilingual.

Meanwhile, as I worked to bridge that divide, I found myself in the middle of many others. I was called in to consult with conservative faith leaders and progressive social-justice activists. I spoke to crowds in rural towns and booming metropolises, in red states and blue. I got to see the inside of other people's echo chambers and to hear what they said when "the other side" wasn't present—and hours later, I might be in a room of people on that other side, listening to them do the exact same thing. The issues these groups raised weren't just about faith and sexuality. They were about race and gender, guns and abortion, personal struggles and public policy—and all sorts of other issues that divide us. These are issues we can't afford to get wrong, and yet I watched as these groups consistently struggled to get through to one another.

We each have issues that matter most to us. You may not be passionate about the faith-sexuality divide like I am—you might even disagree with me entirely—but you have your own positions and issues that are important to you. Maybe there's a political or social topic you'd really like to change some people's minds about. Maybe it's a religious disagreement or even a personal squabble affecting people close to you. But while the specifics of our issues may be different, the principles of communication and change are the same. We need to be able to communicate across our lines of disagreement, but instead, we keep ending up in fights that go nowhere.

Theoretically, we're all fighting for the truth as we see it—and that's reasonable! We *should* do our best for truth, justice, and goodness. Ironically, though, as we fight one another over the truth, the truth is what's being lost. In an echo-chamber world, objective truth carries less weight than truth-as-defined-by-my-social-circles.

What's Led to This Polarization?

In an internet age, it seems like we should be more connected than ever. But in some ways, the very technology that now connects us around the world may be at least partly to blame for pulling us apart.

Before the internet, our social circles were much smaller. Consider someone living in a rural area in the 1950s. Their options for socializing would be mostly limited to their family, their neighbors, and people they knew from school or work. This made it important for that person to find ways to resolve any disputes that arose within those social circles, because without those circles, there weren't a lot of other people to spend time with.

The internet has changed that.

In some ways, that's a really good thing. As a gay teen in an evangelical family, I felt very alone and isolated until I found support on the internet. Lots of people with unique needs or interests have found communities of their own online or even used the internet to find like-minded locals whom they might never have met in their usual social circles. I love the power of the internet to connect people.

But it also comes at a cost. Social media apps make it possible for us to build vast networks of friends and then unceremoniously drop people from our lives the moment we have a dispute. If the person sitting across the table from me says something to irritate me, I can whip out my phone, fire off a message, and get instant sympathy and support from friends around the world who will assure me that of *course* I'm right, and I don't need that person's drama in my life anyway.

And yes, it's great to get support when something bad happens. Sometimes we do need others to encourage us to get away from a bad or abusive relationship. But this also makes it easy for us to give up too quickly on resolving disputes with people who simply see things differently from us.

If you don't agree with my politics, my identity, or my view of the world, I can easily block you or push you away and spend more time with the social circles who affirm what I already believe. That constant stream of approval is intoxicating and addictive. And we don't just get it on social media. We choose news sources, places of worship, and even forms of entertainment that affirm our existing views and demonize *those people out there*. Before we know it, we're living in echo chambers where we hear the same perspectives over and over and over, all of us reinforcing one another in the sense that *we* are the chosen ones, *we* are the "good guys," and the people out there who would oppose us are the enemy.

And it's not that we never interact with *those people*—of course we still do—but we find them making less and less sense to us. We just don't *get* them anymore. They seem incredibly out of touch with reality as we and our social circles know it to be.

And one day, we wake up to find that we're so far apart that we don't even know how to talk to one another anymore.

And we wonder when *they* got like this.

Us-Colored Glasses

It's not just the conscious choices we make that are separating us from one another. There's something else pulling us apart, and many of us aren't even aware of it.

In his 2011 book *The Filter Bubble*, Eli Pariser argued that technology is creating an individually personalized "filter bubble" for each of us—a bubble that filters everything we see on the internet, showing us an altered version of reality based on what computer algorithms think we want.

You and I might both use Google to search for the exact same terms, but we'll get different results. Why? Because Google doesn't just present you with a list of the most popular links. It gives you a list of the information it thinks you *want* based on everything it knows about you, including your location and your past searches.

In an experiment for his book, Pariser asked two friends to each search Google for the term "BP" during that company's much-publicized 2010 oil spill. But even though Pariser's friends were both searching for the same term, what they got back was drastically different. For instance, only one of them saw news about the oil spill in her first page of results, while the other saw investment information. Google's invisible algorithms showed each woman what Google thought she *wanted* to see. With personalized search engines, the same question gives different people different answers.[5]

And that matters, because these days, most of us go to search engines with our most important questions. When we want to know what is true and what isn't, we search online. So if search engines are giving us different answers depending on who's doing the asking, that doesn't help us arrive together at the truth. It just pulls us further apart.

As Pariser puts it:

> With Google personalized for everyone, the query "stem cells" might produce diametrically opposed results for scientists who support stem cell research and activists who oppose it. "Proof of climate change" might turn up different results for an environmental activist and an oil company executive. In polls, a huge majority of us assume search engines are unbiased. But that may be just because they're increasingly biased to share our own views. More and more, your computer monitor is a kind of one-way mirror, reflecting your own interests while algorithmic observers watch what you click.[6]

And this isn't just limited to search engines. You and I could have the same Facebook friends, but we won't see the same posts when we log on. Like Google, Facebook shows us what it thinks we want to see, based on accumulated data like what we've clicked in the past.

This means that social media sites like Facebook can doubly skew our view of the world. We're starting from a biased sample to begin with, because the news we see on Facebook is determined by who our Facebook friends are, and most of us tend to have Facebook friends who are similar to us and who agree with us on the issues we care about most. Sure, you probably don't agree with *all* your Facebook friends on *everything*, but most people's Facebook friend lists are skewed in the direction of being like them in terms of race, religion, location, socioeconomic status, political views, and so on.

But even if your friends were purely representative—a cross-section of the world—you still wouldn't get an unbiased view from Facebook, because you don't see everything your friends post. You see only the things Facebook thinks you *want* to see. If you click more on political articles that lean right, Facebook will show you more political articles that lean right. If you never click on political articles that lean right, Facebook will start showing you something else instead, and that viewpoint will be gradually erased from your Facebook view of the world.

Even if you don't get your news from Facebook or other social media, a lot of people do—Facebook had more than two billion active users in 2017, and that's just one of a number of growing social networks where people share news and ideas, all with similar problems.[7] It's not just social media, either. Our news and information landscape is increasingly splintered, making it easier for all of us to hear a version of the truth catered to our own personal biases.

Until a few years ago, the members of a community generally got their news from the same sources of information. We watched the nightly news as a nation; we read the local newspaper. Today, many television news programs target viewers with a particular viewpoint and present the news accordingly, while an increasing number of us get our news from social media and partisan news websites—and, in some cases, clickbait websites that intentionally peddle made-up news stories designed for maximum shock and outrage.

In 2016, the *Wall Street Journal* built "Blue Feed, Red Feed," an internet project designed to demonstrate how Democrats and Republicans are further polarized by the ways our preferred news sources present the facts (or, in some cases, the *different* facts they choose to present).[8] The Blue Feed, Red Feed webpage, run by a computer algorithm, presents two imaginary news feeds side by side—one showing recent articles from news sources preferred by liberals, the other showing articles on the same topic from news sources preferred by conservatives. The differences are stark. As I was writing this chapter, for example, I pulled up the site to see what the different feeds had to say about guns. The Blue Feed featured headlines like "NYPD Guns Down Yet Another Black Person in Mental Distress, This Time in Brooklyn, NY," while the Red Feed featured headlines like "NY Deputies Knock on Veteran's Door, Tell Him He's Mentally Ill and Confiscate His Guns—They Were Wrong."

Is it any wonder we see one another as living in totally different realities? We get a biased assortment of links from our social media feeds, we turn to biased sources of information to learn more, and then we go back to our biased social bubbles where people affirm what we just learned.

We're no longer having a single national conversation on the issues that shape our lives, and that has devastating consequences for all of us.

And yet, even as this problem has become clear, the solution has not. Journalists, tech experts, and political pundits have written to decry the contribution of fake news and personalized news feeds to American polarization, but they do so from within their own bubbles—able to see that there's "another America" out there but unsure how to realistically move beyond their own echo chamber and have a meaningful impact in someone else's. If we really want to address this divide, we need fluency on both sides of the aisle and the ability to translate ideas between them. But too often, that fluency just isn't there. Even when we know certain people well as individuals, we don't understand their echo chambers well enough to change their minds on the things we care about, so we end up surprised when they're not persuaded by arguments that seem obvious to us. Each side is so focused on *fighting* the other that there doesn't seem to be any room for *understanding* them. As a result, each side unwittingly sabotages their own efforts to change the other side's mind.

Somehow, we've got to get through to one another.

This book is about how *you* can do it—one conversation at a time.

CHAPTER 2

But I Can't Talk to Those People!

The world would be way easier if other people's OPINIONS
weren't so INCORRECT all the time.

—T-Rex, from Ryan North's *Dinosaur Comics*[9]

It's easy to say that we should try to reach across our cultural divides.

But I'll admit it: Some days, I prefer to stay in my bubble.

There are days when I'm browsing my social media feeds, or chatting with a friend, or even just out at the store, when someone says something that I find frustrating and offensive and *just plain wrong*—but I don't want to get into a disagreement, so I don't say anything. Some days, I just don't want to deal with any of it. I want to be surrounded only by people who *get it*. In those moments, that bubble sounds like a perfect world.

It's understandable that people long for bubbles when they're frustrated. A week after Donald Trump's election, *Saturday Night Live* satirically invited disaffected progressives to join "the Bubble . . . a planned community of like-minded freethinkers—and no one else. So if you're an open-minded person, come here and close yourself in." Brutal. Yet even in *SNL*'s fictional Bubble, not everyone is on the same page. "We don't see color here. But we cel-ebrate it," smarms a smiling white guy—as an African American woman next to him gives the camera a look of resigned irritation.[10]

On the other side of the aisle, I grew up in a very different kind of bubble. In my conservative evangelical church, the as-sumption was that every good Christian voted Republican; I was at least twenty before I heard anyone use the word "liberal" in anything other than a derogatory sense. I listened to evangelical radio, read evangelical magazines, and bought all my music at the Christian bookstore across town. When I finally bought my first "secular" album as a teenager—an innocuous bit of silliness by college-rock band They Might Be Giants—I was almost afraid to listen to it, concerned that music from outside my evangelical bubble might somehow be laced with evil.

Today, I have friends who live in a real-world version of *SNL*'s progressive bubble and friends who live in a conservative evan-gelical bubble like the one I grew up in. I also have friends in many other bubbles—religious, social, geographic, ideological. And I have unique, very specific bubbles of my own—tiny bub-bles comprised only of people with similar life experiences where I feel like everyone gets me. Your bubbles might be similar to mine, or they might be very different.

But as comforting as it is to retreat from a frustrating world and hide in our bubbles, we can't allow ourselves to live there. Isolating ourselves only makes the problem worse.

Isolating ourselves only makes the problem worse.

The issues you care about, the problems in the outside world that make you long for the reassurance of your bubble, cannot be resolved solely from within your bubble. If you want to see people's hearts and minds change on the things that matter to you, more people like *you* are going to have to speak up and be heard. You're going to have to reach beyond your bubble—beyond your echo chamber—and speak into someone else's.

Otherwise, we're all in big trouble.

The Danger of Echo Chambers

If you've ever taken a psychology class, you've probably heard about a famous 1951 study by Solomon Asch.[11] Asch put a group of male college students in a room together and gave them a series of visual tests. They were asked to answer questions aloud about which of three lines—labeled A, B, and C—was the same size as a fourth, unlabeled line. The tests were simple, and the answers were easy to determine. When tested alone, subjects named the correct line more than 99 percent of the time.

But in the group setting, there was a catch: Only one of the young men in the room was actually a subject in the experiment. Unbeknownst to him, all the other "subjects" were secretly in league with the researcher and had been told to lie, all giving the same wrong answer on certain questions. Asch's real experiment was to determine the influence of the group: If everyone else gave an answer that was obviously wrong, would the subject go along with the group, or would he defy the majority and give the correct answer?

As it turned out, most subjects (75 percent) gave an obviously wrong answer in order to conform with the majority opinion at least once during the experiment. When Asch interviewed them later, some said that they'd known the answer was wrong, but others insisted that they'd *actually believed the lie.*

Real-life echo chambers are more complex than Asch's simple experiment, but the experiment is a great illustration of the tremendous power our social circles have to sway how we behave and even what we believe. When we hear something over and over from the people around us, we begin to buy into it. The more we hear it, the more reasonable it seems and the harder it can be for people outside our echo chambers to change our minds.

Surround a person with enough people who all say line A is the answer, and that person eventually starts to believe it—even if their eyes tell them differently.

Millions of people out in the world would have known the right answer at a glance. But inside the echo chamber, all that mattered were the other voices in the room.

If peer pressure is strong enough to change people's minds when the answer is obvious, just imagine what that kind of pressure can do on issues where the answer is less obvious. And if outside views don't eventually make their way in, the problem gets even worse. Echo chambers don't just nurture conformity; they can also nurture extremism.

Research has repeatedly shown that if a group of like-minded people are put in a room together and allowed to discuss an issue where they all tend to lean in the same direction, their constant affirmation of one another's views can cause the group as a whole to become *more extreme*. Perhaps in the beginning they started out mildly preferring option 1 over option 2, but after hearing one another sing the praises of option 1, they can end up much more strongly in favor of option 1 than any of them were at the start. This "group polarization" effect has been seen so often that researchers Helmut Lamm and David G. Myers wrote that "seldom in the history of social psychology has a nonobvious phenomenon been so firmly grounded in data from across a variety of cultures and dependent measures."[12]

Echo chambers are the enemy of the truth. They tear apart communities and stifle communication. And in our society, they're growing ever more powerful.

But here's the good news: Echo chambers aren't absolute. Most of Asch's subjects *did* defy the majority at least once, and Asch found that simply bringing one other person into the room with the correct answer made it far more likely that they would do so. A single outside voice can be incredibly powerful in countering the effects of an echo chamber.

You can be that voice. All it takes is a willingness to talk to people in other bubbles about the issues that matter to you.

Talking to a Brick Wall

"But wait," you say. "I've *tried* talking to those people. I get *no-where*."

I know the feeling. Talking about major disagreements with some people can feel like talking to a brick wall—or running face-first into one. But I've noticed that the brick wall feeling is usually caused by the same five barriers popping up over and over in conversations with different people. These five barriers—things like *misinformation* and *team loyalty*—are what stand between you and the other person and make those conversations so difficult.

The brick wall feeling is usually caused by the same five barriers.

In the pages ahead, I'll teach you strategies to break down the five barriers and give you the best chance of being heard by people in other bubbles. But for any strategy to be effective, you have to put it into practice. You can't just read this book the way you might read a novel—just a bit of pleasure reading—if you want it to be effective. I encourage you to take your time with the ideas in this book, thinking deeply about how they relate to specific people and issues in your own life. Try out the techniques and principles in real conversations and see what challenges you run into. Don't let these concepts remain theoretical for you.

TALKING ACROSS THE DIVIDE

Thanksgiving with Uncle John

Picture it: You're having Thanksgiving dinner with your extended family. You've deftly avoided a series of prying questions from Aunt Gertrude about your personal life, and you're helping yourself to another serving of mashed potatoes when Uncle John suddenly speaks up.

"Did you hear the news about—?"

Before he's finished the sentence, you already know the issue he's going to raise. It's an issue you care about deeply, and you know he's on the other side of it. You've heard his rants before—rambling, uninformed, assuming everyone else agrees with him. You *don't* agree with him *at all*, but you also don't want to cause a scene. You clench your teeth and wonder if you'll make it through this meal without losing your temper.

At parties, on social media, at work, and at dinner, opportunities to talk to "those people"—the ones you disagree with most—are all around if you watch for them. The question is, what do you do when they arise?

Most of us really have only three main tools in our toolbox when it comes to handling these sorts of disagreements: We fight, we avoid, or we compromise.

If an issue is important to us, our first instinct is usually to *fight*. We argue to try to convince the other side to see things our way, and if that doesn't work, we escalate: We get louder, we add pressure, we threaten negative consequences if the other side doesn't do what we want.

If we don't want to fight or can't get what we want through fighting, we may choose to *avoid* the disagreement. Many friendships and family relationships have been saved by simply "agreeing to disagree" and choosing not to raise the subject again. Sometimes, that's the best thing to do; there's no reason to lose a friend over a minor squabble. In more extreme cases, we might decide to cut the other person or people out of our life entirely and avoid the disagreement that way. That can be necessary for our own sanity, but relying on that approach too often is what creates a polarized world.

However, there are many situations in life where fighting and avoidance don't work. And most of us have been taught only one other way of handling those disputes: *compromise*. You want $15,000 for the car, I'm willing to pay $11,000, so, okay, let's meet in the middle at $13,000, as long as you'll throw in those floor mats.

Compromise is simple; we understand compromise. But what if an issue is too important to compromise on? What if only one party is at fault and the other is being harmed? What if there simply is no middle ground? In situations like these, many of us don't know what to do. Once compromise is ruled out, we don't have many other tools in our toolbox, and so we go back to some combination of fighting and/or avoidance. We argue, threaten, pressure, and do whatever else we can to get our way while simultaneously cutting people out of our lives when we can't convince them. We end up in our own bubbles, certain we're right, surrounded by people who encourage us and help us lob grenades at the other side. We know *those people* are still out there, and in many cases, we know they're out there doing harm. But we have no idea how to make them listen to us, so we sit and stew in our own frustration.

From time to time, maybe one of *them* will post something on our social media feeds or in the comments of a website we visit, and we'll argue with them for a while. Maybe one of them will bring something up at a family gathering, and we'll try in vain to make them see the light. But at the end of the day, nothing ever seems to change, and after a while we just block them and shut them out, exhausted from trying to get through their thick skulls.

We need a fourth tool.

CHAPTER 3

The Fourth Tool

We have to face the fact that either all of us are going to die together or we are going to learn to live together—and if we live together, we have to talk.

—Eleanor Roosevelt[13]

A few years ago, I organized a public dialogue event on a college campus in a deeply conservative, heavily evangelical part of the country. The topic of the event was homosexuality and Christianity, a pairing that had already proven controversial on that campus and many others like it. In a series of one-on-one conversations and surveys prior to the event, it had become clear that the students were very divided. A fair number of members of the LGBT student group had come from Christian homes, but many had since left their parents' faith, and most were deeply distrustful of the Christian groups on campus.* Meanwhile, many mem-

---

*At the time of the event, the term "LGBT" (lesbian, gay, bisexual, and transgender) was being widely used to describe sexual and gender minorities. As I write this, it's still the most widely known term, so I've used it throughout the book for consistency, but I also want to recognize that some groups do not feel adequately represented by this term and there is an ongoing push to change it, with variants like LGBTQ and LGBTQIA becoming more widely used.

bers of those Christian groups, particularly those who identified as conservative or Evangelical, likewise expressed deep suspicion of the LGBT group and its motives. Both groups privately expressed feeling misunderstood and unfairly maligned.

As the event began, the tension in the auditorium was palpable. Students chatted nervously, eyeing one another across the room, some thumbing through bookmarked Bible pages and notes they had brought with them. They were prepared for a fight.

I opened the event with a few words about my own background and the nature of productive dialogue, established some ground rules, and then opened the floor for people to ask honest questions of those they disagreed with. I carefully moderated the discussion, occasionally stepping in to reframe a question, but mostly, I wanted these students to hear one another.

And when the event ended ninety minutes later, something remarkable had changed. Members of the different groups intermingled and chatted animatedly, asking one another for contact information and offering to get together more often in the future. A group of students from both sides asked if I would join them for dinner afterward to continue the conversation. For the next couple of hours, I listened to them tell their stories, laugh together, and talk about ways to create more dialogue on their campus.

Here were LGBT students and conservative evangelical Christians—two groups not known for getting along—going to dinner together, adding each other on Facebook, seeing each other as people worth getting to know. And, incredibly, all of this had been accomplished not by *ignoring* their disagreements but by actually *talking* about them and truly listening to each other. This wasn't some veneer of politeness for the sake of society. This was a genuine breakthrough on both sides. It was real, honest communication.

Imagine if we could make that happen between all the polarized groups in our society! Just think of all the good we could accomplish.

What's more, this wasn't an isolated incident. I did similar events on more than twenty campuses across the country, and I saw the same kinds of things happen over and over, at one school after another.

So what made the difference? Why is it that these events succeeded when countless other attempts to talk across the same divide have failed so miserably?

This wasn't just a fluke. These events were carefully planned with a specific method in mind—a method I've used in one-on-one conversations and in messages for audiences of all sizes with similarly encouraging results. It's an approach that can help you get through to the people *you* want to reach, whoever they are.

If you keep the basic principles of this method in mind, you can break down the barriers to understanding, combat our cultural echo chambers, and, in many cases, change hearts and minds that you thought could never be changed.

Together, these principles make up our missing fourth tool— *strategic dialogue.*

Not All Dialogue Is Created Equal

"Oh. I see."

I find that most people have a fairly underwhelming reaction to the word "dialogue." It sounds wishy-washy in all the worst ways. Fight for what's right? Sure. Crush the opposition? Absolutely. But *dialogue*? It sounds like the sort of useless, hopelessly idealistic thinking that might have prompted your mom to suggest you just *talk* to the bully on the playground and *make friends*. Yes, dialogue's a nice idea and all, and maybe it's fine for some situations, but, buddy, this is the real world and there are real villains doing real damage where real lives may hang in the balance. Any self-proclaimed self-help guru can tell you to talk things out. But, to paraphrase one of Sia's album titles, some of us have *real* problems. Recommending dialogue as a solution to world polarization sounds a bit like offering a baby aspirin to someone with a migraine.

I get this kind of reaction all the time.

Before the word "dialogue" comes up, I actually have some pretty interesting conversations with people. I'll be flying on a plane for a speaking engagement, or making casual conversation at a social gathering, when someone asks me what I do. When I mention my work at the intersection of faith and sexuality, I get a lot of different responses. Some people don't care—it's not a topic that particularly interests them. Others, however, care a lot, and as soon as I raise the topic, they're instantly trying to size me up, to figure out whether I'm on *their side* or the *other side*.

If they suspect I might be on the *other side*, I can tell right away. Their whole demeanor changes. They close themselves off, narrow their eyes, and become much less talkative—or they shift into debate mode, asking me leading questions and telling me what they think.

On the other hand, if they assume I'm on *their side*—whichever "side" that is—they'll often start to open up right away, telling me how glad they are that I'm out there doing the good work of showing *those people* the truth. *Those people* are so ignorant, they say. *Those people* are so wrong. Thank goodness I'm out there setting those people straight . . . so to speak.

But that enthusiasm dwindles when I mention that my work involves a form of dialogue with both sides. People who were thrilled just moments before at the idea of going out to *fight* the other side are much less excited to *dialogue* with them. And I can understand why. "Dialogue" sounds weak. It sounds like a way of legitimizing a viewpoint that might actually be wrong and harmful. "Enough talk," they say. "It's time for action." Dialogue is often treated as the opposite of action, and with so much at stake, the idea that I promote dialogue is deeply disappointing to them.

Perhaps you feel that way about dialogue, too. It's all well and good to have a bunch of people in an auditorium listen to one another and go to dinner together, but how does that help you when you're trying to resolve a conflict with a stubborn relative? How does it help a minority group whose rights are being stomped on or a lone crusader fighting for what's right against a tidal wave of opposition?

"I want more than that," you may be saying. "I'm not trying to get a bunch of people to make friends and have a conversation. I want to change someone's mind. It doesn't do me any good if we sit around talking and getting to know each other but no one actually changes their opinion. I *already* know plenty of people I disagree with, and that's enough to drive me crazy as it is!"

If that's what you're thinking, I hear you. And that's why "strategic dialogue" must be *strategic*. Unfortunately, there's a lot of unproductive, non-strategic dialogue out there that's, frankly, pretty useless when it comes to changing attitudes. Strategic dialogue is different.

What Is Strategic Dialogue?

In this book, I'll be using the term "strategic dialogue" to refer to a particular way of communicating with people you disagree with—whether that's a single family member or a national movement. It's a technique designed to reduce tension, change attitudes, and remove obstacles to the truth. When used properly, strategic dialogue is a powerful tool for changing minds on even the most controversial and divisive issues.

Think of someone you have trouble getting through to—someone who just won't listen to you even when you've got a strong logical case for your position. Well, *there's a reason they're not listening.* People aren't always logical, and we all have certain psychological barriers that can get in the way of seeing the truth for what it is. Strategic dialogue is about breaking through those barriers to create pathways of understanding, allowing both sides to see things more clearly.

There's a reason they're not listening.

Strategic dialogue is *not* about manipulating or tricking someone into believing what you want them to. There are no sleazy sales tactics here, and there's no guarantee that the other person will change their mind—especially if your case turns out not to be as strong as you thought it was. But in situations where egos, polarization, and lies are clouding people's judgment, strategic dialogue offers the most effective way to clear all that away.

Basic Principles of Strategic Dialogue

Before we start digging into the nitty-gritty, let's take a minute to look at four fundamental truths about strategic dialogue and how it operates.

1. Everyone thinks they're right.

This should be self-evident, but it's surprisingly easy to forget. Even if you're sure "those people" are wrong, *they* think they're right. That affects how they behave and how they'll respond to you.

2. We want to change each other's minds.

Just because everyone *thinks* they're right doesn't mean everyone *is* right. Sometimes, people are wrong. So let's just admit it: If you think I'm wrong about something, then you probably want to change my mind. Likewise, I want to change yours.

This is important, because a lot of people think "dialogue" means never taking sides, just talking about our differing beliefs and refusing to label anyone's views as "wrong" or "damaging."

"Everyone is right in their own way!" this unhelpful dialogue says. "All views are valid; we all have our own truth!"

In real life, everyone can't always be right.

But in real life, everyone can't always be right. Not all views are valid. If someone wants to deny the Holocaust or claims that people of a certain race are inferior, that's not okay; that's not a "valid viewpoint."

There *are* questions where everyone's opinion is equally valid. There's no right or wrong answer to a question like "What's the best ice-cream flavor?" Everyone has a right to argue for the merits of their own personal favorite (although I will never understand those of you who choose butter pecan).

But often, the issues we fight over are issues where getting the answer right makes a huge difference. In some cases, lives are literally at stake. Is climate change threatening the future of the planet? Is hell real, and are some people in danger of going there? Does gun control make us safer—or less safe? Could a change in school policy help curb bullying and save kids' lives? On issues like these, people get upset because *there's so much at stake*. Getting it right *matters*. So if I'm confident I know what the right answer is, I'm going to fight as hard as I can to convince you, because I care about the outcome. I want to change your mind—and you probably want to change mine.

3. Dialogue is more effective than debate at changing minds.

It's counterintuitive, but it's true: While it seems most natural to reach for debate or argument to change someone's mind, those approaches are actually *less* likely to get the results you want.

To understand why, take a moment to think back to the last heated argument you were in.

Who was it with? What was it about? How did it make you feel? How did it end?

As well as you can, try to put yourself back into that place in the midst of that argument. Were you defensive? Angry? Embarrassed? Frustrated? Did you feel like the other person understood where you were coming from or not? Why did you feel that way?

In the heat of that argument, how were you feeling about the other person and the case they were making? Did they change your mind? Why or why not?

There's something weird about arguments: They're the first thing we reach for when we want to change someone's mind, and yet they're not very effective at actually changing minds. The more desperate we are to change someone's mind, the more passionately we argue. And the more passionately we argue, the more defensive each side gets. It's as if we're trying to force them into our way of thinking by making our words louder and harsher, but in so doing, we only cause them to dig in their heels more and more, as both sides grow increasingly angry and irrational.

It's like the so-called Chinese finger trap—a tube-shaped toy that connects to one finger on each hand. The more you try to pull the fingers away from each other and out of the trap, the more the trap tightens around them. The force we use by instinct turns out to be our enemy. Instead, the only way to free your fingers from the trap is, paradoxically, by pushing them closer together and farther into the trap.

Arguments are like that. The tension we generate by arguing with someone makes them only more resistant to our case. And calling it a "debate" instead of an "argument" doesn't make it much more effective. People often still get emotional—or may even get angry that you're *not* getting emotional about a subject they care about. If we want to have the best chance of getting them to listen to us, we need to find a way to lower that tension.

Even if you are successful at having a completely logical debate and it doesn't get heated at any point, debates still aren't very good at changing the participants' minds, because in a debate, each person's goal is to *win*.

Imagine that you and I are debating about some issue where we strongly disagree. I've got a brilliant argument that I can't wait to throw at you, because I'm sure that you won't be able to counter it, so the whole time you're making your argument, I'm plotting the moment to throw my brilliant argument at you. Finally, the moment arrives, and I make my brilliant argument, the one I'm sure will blow you out of the water.

But it doesn't. Why? Well, because the whole time I'm making my supposedly brilliant argument, you're busy thinking about your rebuttal, trying to find the best ways to poke holes in my argument so that *you* can win the debate. In the midst of a debate, we're not actually listening to each other very well, at least not in the way you'd need to listen to consider new points of view. We're only listening so that we can counter each other, and with that kind of approach, it's very unlikely that either of us is going to be swayed. If anything, we're just going to wind up further apart than we started.

The solution is to talk about our disagreements in a way that encourages listening and breaks down barriers instead of putting them up. That's why strategic dialogue can win people over when debate and argument fail.

4. Finally, dialogue isn't a substitute for action.

We can all think of situations throughout history and in our own lives when *action* was required to stop a conflict or make change. Sometimes it takes civil disobedience, protests, or legal pressure to get people to do the right thing. Sometimes even war is inevitable. And certainly, if you're in an abusive relationship, you need to take action and get out of that relationship.

When people first hear me talk about strategic dialogue as a response to our divisions, some mistakenly assume that I'm proposing a world where they allow the other side to walk all over them and perpetuate injustice, all while hoping that *feel-good conversation* will magically save the day.

No, no, no.

There are times when certain actions must be taken for the sake of what's right. If someone is harming you or others, you can't wait for them to realize the error of their ways before you take the necessary steps to protect those in need. Depending on the situation, that might mean standing up to a bully, lobbying a legislator, calling for a boycott, or doing whatever other action is reasonable and necessary to help stop something wrong from being done.

But in all of this, there's an important role for *diplomacy*.

You can't have a war or a lawsuit or a protest every time someone's in the wrong. If you do, you soon become the bully, imposing your will on everyone else through force. There are also many situations where things like protests don't work. Sometimes they can even backfire, turning your opponents into martyrs for their cause. In cases like these, dialogue can often accomplish what actions cannot.

Even when these sorts of actions *are* necessary, adding diplomacy can make them far more effective and help you accomplish more of what you want more quickly. It's true that negative consequences like a boycott or a threat of public shaming can force people to change their actions in the short term. But if they're only changing their actions to avoid something negative, the change can be short-lived, and resentment can build in the meantime. People trying to avoid negative consequences tend to do the bare minimum required and then change back to their old ways as soon as they think they can get away with it.

Strategic dialogue, on the other hand, helps create lasting *attitude* change—and when people's attitudes change, they become your allies, not just people you've beaten into temporary, begrudging submission.

So with these principles in mind, let's dive into the step-by-step strategy of using dialogue to change attitudes on the issues that most matter to you.

An Overview of Strategic Dialogue

My childhood copy of the board game Othello advertised itself with the slogan "A minute to learn . . . A lifetime to master." Strategic dialogue is a lot like that. At its most basic level, strategic dialogue is just about using skills you already have—skills like listening and telling stories—to communicate with people you disagree with. In that sense, it's surprisingly simple. But the *strategy* of when and how to use these skills is what gives this technique its power. And in that sense, it really does take a lifetime to master.

BASIC STEPS OF STRATEGIC DIALOGUE

A. PREPARATION (CHAPTER 4)

STEP 1   PREPARE YOURSELF.

STEP 2   PREPARE YOUR AUDIENCE.

STEP 3   PREPARE THE SPACE.

B. DIALOGUE (CHAPTERS 5–13)

STEP 4   USE STRATEGIC LISTENING.

STEP 5   USE STRATEGIC STORYTELLING.

STEP 6   REPEAT TO BREAK DOWN BARRIERS.

C. NEXT STEPS (CHAPTERS 14–16)

STEP 7   MAKE AN ASK.

STEP 8   REFLECT AND EVALUATE.

STEP 9   REPEAT PROCESS.

There are three phases to a strategic dialogue: Preparation, Dialogue, and Next Steps.

During the Preparation phase, you'll make some key decisions and ensure that both you and your dialogue partner(s) are ready for a productive dialogue. We'll talk more about this in the next chapter.

The Dialogue phase is where you'll do the majority of the work, and it makes up the majority of this book. The goal of this phase is to break down four of the major barriers that stand in the way of your message being heard: ego protection, team loyalty, comfort, and misinformation.

Finally, in the Next Steps phase, you'll address the fifth barrier—worldview protection—and work to ensure that your dialogue has a clear, measurable outcome that helps you make progress toward your goal.

Keep in mind that strategic dialogue is an art form, not a magic formula. You might not always use every step or follow every suggestion, and that's okay. I've included concrete details like these to make it easier to understand how strategic dialogue works. But don't let that confine or overwhelm you. Everyone is different, and real-life situations can be unpredictable, so don't be afraid to experiment and tweak to make the process work for you.

CHAPTER 4

How to Prepare for a Successful Dialogue

I . . . never could make a good impromptu speech without
several hours to prepare it.
—Mark Twain[14]

_____

So you've got an issue you want to discuss or a person you want to get through to. Great! (If you don't have anyone in mind yet, try to think of someone now. This book will be more meaningful if you're thinking of real situations.) But before you rush right into a dialogue, there are some things you can do to make your dialogue go much more smoothly.

Step 1: Prepare Yourself

Getting strategic dialogue right takes planning. It's a lot like business meetings: Anyone can call a meeting, but it takes effort and intentionality to make a meeting *productive*. I've been in plenty of pointless meetings where nothing significant was accomplished, and I always want to say, "Why did I spend an hour of my life in this meeting just to learn something I could have read about in five minutes in an email?" Pointless meetings are the *worst*.

The best meetings are energizing and productive—and, unfortunately, all too rare. Ask any management consultant what makes the difference between a fantastic meeting and a terrible meeting, and I can almost guarantee that they'll talk about the importance of *preparation*. Well-run meetings are well-planned meetings. It takes time and effort in advance to make the best use of the time.

Dialogue is the same way. I've had to sit through a lot of terrible attempts at dialogue where people just talked and talked and talked but nothing ever came out of it, no one's mind was changed on anything, and participants wound up feeling as though they'd just wasted their time. Strategic dialogue should have *goals* and make an *impact* on people. To accomplish that, you need to prepare yourself for the dialogue long before the dialogue begins.

Learn about the issues at stake.

First, make sure you understand the issues at stake as well as possible. You don't want to be in the middle of your dialogue when you suddenly realize you don't know what you're talking about! Take the time to research all sides of your issue. If possible, you want to be able to explain clearly what the other side believes and why they believe it.

Research all sides of your issue.

Let's say you're in favor of a proposed anti-bullying policy at your kids' school, but there's been some resistance. As you prepare for the dialogue, ask yourself: Why *wouldn't* everyone want the anti-bullying policy? Do some research, and see if you can answer that question before you even sit down to talk. Do people think the proposal is ineffective? That it would waste resources? That it would infringe on their beliefs? See what objections have been discussed online or in local news media.

The better you understand the strengths and weaknesses of *both* sides, the better equipped you will be to represent your position well in this dialogue.

Decide on your goal.

What would you like to accomplish? Think about the issue at hand and what you could realistically imagine a successful outcome to be.

With the college dialogue event, I had fairly modest goals. I wanted to spark ongoing communication between the LGBT community and the Christian community—groups who had been fighting for years without actually talking to each other. I also particularly wanted Evangelicals who grew up like I did to understand the negative impact of their words and actions on their LGBT peers. My goal, then, was to build understanding and a sense of shared community between these two campus groups. That was as much as I felt I could accomplish in one meeting, but I hoped it would lead to more conversation and an attitude change in the long run. (I'm told that it has.)

In a similar vein, your goal might be to restore a damaged relationship or change someone's general attitude toward an issue that matters to you. It doesn't have to be any more than that. On the other hand, you might have a more concrete goal, such as getting people to vote a certain way on an issue or to alter their behavior. I've used strategic dialogue to work for specific policy changes in universities and churches, for instance, or to convince parents not to force their kids into reorientation therapy. Whatever your goal is, make sure it's clear in your mind from the beginning. You can't make progress on something without a sense of the direction you'd like to go.

Get to know your audience.

With your goal in mind, spend some time thinking about your audience. If you'll be dialoguing with someone you don't know well, take some time to learn about them in advance. Do they have a blog, published writings, or even public social media accounts that could help you learn about their values? Take advantage of that. The more you know about what they believe and what's important to them, the easier it will be to speak to them on their level.

Most of the time, you'll already know at this point who your audience is. But in some cases, you have multiple options, and this is when you'll need to decide who to sit down with. If your issue is the school anti-bullying policy, you might talk to other parents to help build a groundswell of support, or you might meet with the principal, or you might talk to influential members of the school board. You could even do all of these. Consider the options you have and decide where you think you have the best chance of making an impact.

Until you get very comfortable with strategic dialogue, I strongly suggest focusing on *one-on-one* dialogue. Group dialogue can be more easily derailed and is generally more difficult to manage, and one-on-one dialogue is often the most effective anyway. If there are multiple people whose minds you'd like to change, it will probably be easier to do with a series of one-on-one conversations rather than having everyone in a room together. As you get used to the process, you'll find there are many ways to adapt it for larger groups, if that's something you decide to pursue later on.

Get ready emotionally.

Strategic dialogue isn't always easy. It requires keeping your temper in check and being willing to hold your tongue when all you want to do is argue. It's often unfair, requiring you to be the "bigger person" even if something is the other person's fault.

So in addition to the intellectual preparation, spend some time preparing yourself *emotionally* for the challenges ahead. Envision yourself responding peacefully to ignorant or frustrating things the other person might say.

Make sure you're prepared for the worst, but hope for the best: Try not to imagine the other person as your enemy but as a potential ally who might surprise you with how well they respond to the dialogue. And remember, if things don't go well, you can always walk away from the dialogue if you need to.

Step 2: Prepare Your Audience

When you invite someone to dialogue with you, the *way* you invite them is going to set the stage for the kind of conversation you have. You want this conversation to be as friendly and relaxed as possible, no matter how much you disagree, so your invitation needs to reflect that.

The nature of your invitation depends a lot on your relationship with the person you're talking to. If you want to dialogue with your university president, you'll probably need to make an appointment and get on her or his calendar. If you want a dialogue with your sister, though, your invitation should be much more informal: "Hey Char, do you want to get some ice cream and continue that conversation about gender politics?" Whatever form your invitation takes, use this as an opportunity to prepare your audience for what's to come.

Set the stage for productive dialogue.

As I mentioned in the previous chapter, a lot of people have a negative reaction to the idea of "dialogue." When you invite someone to meet with you and talk about an issue you disagree on, you may know what you have in mind, but they don't. They might think you want to argue with them, or lecture them, or spring something on them to make them look foolish. This worry might cause them to turn down your invitation or to show up in the wrong frame of mind.

It's important to set expectations right from the beginning.

To prevent this kind of misunderstanding, it's important to *set expectations* right from the beginning—to clarify what you mean by "dialogue" and what you hope to accomplish.

Don't talk about it as an opportunity for *you* to tell *them* what they should do or why you disagree with them. No one wants to make time to be lectured, and if they do, they're going to show up with all their emotional armor on, ready to fight rather than to listen.

Instead, make clear that you want to hear *their* perspective on the issue and that you'd like to discuss the situation and work on a way forward *together*. Part of the dialogue process involves giving them uninterrupted time to share their thoughts—so make sure they know that going in.

Every time I run a public dialogue event, I always begin with a quick explanation of what dialogue *is* and *isn't*: It *isn't* saying "everyone is equally right," and it *isn't* debate or argument. It *is* a chance to hear one another out and seek to build understanding while acknowledging that we still want to change one another's minds.

After these events, I've had a number of people come up to me to say that the moment I clearly set those expectations was the moment they first felt able to relax and let down their guard a bit. For people to feel comfortable in a dialogue, they need to know what to expect and that they will be treated respectfully. They also need to know that you're not asking them to gloss over genuine areas of disagreement.

For instance: "Bob, I know there's been a lot of tension between us ever since that argument a few months ago, and I hate that, because I really value our relationship. I know this is important to both of us, and I know we still disagree. I'm sure you'd like to change my mind as much as I'd still like to change yours. But I'm also realizing that I've never really given you uninterrupted time to share your side of things, and I'd like to do that, to really hear you out. And then, if you're open to it, maybe I could share my side, too. I know we'll probably still end up disagreeing, but I would feel better knowing that at least we've cleared the air and can understand each other a bit better."

Give them a reason to take the time.

Even if you don't say it explicitly, your invitation also needs to give the other person a reason to care enough to show up. Think about what they could get out of the dialogue that would be useful or valuable to them.

If you have a personal relationship with them, perhaps their motivation might be to help reduce the tension in the relationship by spending time listening to one another. If they have a view they're eager to share, perhaps their motivation might be to create an atmosphere where *you* are willing to listen to *them*. If you're talking to someone in a public position—such as if you're representing a group of unhappy constituents talking to a politician or an organization's leadership—their motivation might be to smooth things over and avoid public controversy.

There are lots and lots of reasons someone might be motivated to dialogue. The question you have to ask yourself is: What does *this* person want, and what would be valuable about this dialogue for them? If you can't think of any reason they'd find the dialogue valuable—anything they want that a successful dialogue could bring them—then you probably won't be able to convince them to take the time.

Step 3: Prepare the Space

Once you actually sit down to dialogue, it's important to have a space that makes it easy to have nuanced conversation. Again, this is something you want to plan in advance.

Find a relaxing environment.
If it's possible, plan for a way to talk without interruptions—no cell phones, no screaming kids, just a relaxing space where you can talk for a while. (If that's not possible, get as close to that as you can.) Take them out for coffee or dessert—your treat—or plan some time around a mindless activity you know they enjoy, such as a walk in the park. You want them to be comfortable opening up, and you don't want to be interrupted in the middle of a thought.

Set ground rules.

Just as it's important to set expectations in your invitation, you want to reiterate those expectations in some way when you sit down to dialogue. And, especially if there's tension between you, it can help to agree on some simple ground rules, like being willing to listen to each other, avoid interrupting, and do your best to try to understand each other's perspective.

In a one-on-one setting, you don't have to do this as formally as I did in the auditorium—you probably don't want to pull out a whiteboard and write out "Ground Rules"—but you do need to take a moment to clarify what you're asking for. Acknowledge that you disagree and that you probably both would like to change each other's minds on some things—and focus on the power of dialogue to help you understand each other. You might also talk about what you hope to get out of the conversation and/or what you think they might be happy to gain from the conversation.

What If You Don't Have Time to Prepare?

Of course, as important as this prep work is, you may sometimes find yourself in a situation that is ripe for dialogue even though you haven't had a chance to prepare in advance. Maybe you're at a party when a total stranger strikes up a conversation with you about an issue you care about, and it's now or never. That's okay! You can still use strategic-dialogue techniques even in situations where you can't follow every step perfectly. Remember, strategic dialogue is an art form, not a magic formula. As you practice it, you'll find a number of occasions where things don't go quite according to plan and you have to adapt the technique to the situation. The more comfortable you get with strategic dialogue, the easier that will be.

Once you've done whatever preparation you're able to do, it's time to move into the heart of the dialogue, beginning with a practice that is incredibly simple—and one of the most important things you can do in any strategic dialogue.

CHAPTER 5

Shut Up and Listen

Listen now. When people talk listen completely. Don't be thinking what you're going to say. Most people never listen.
—Ernest Hemingway[15]

As a young man, I worked for a couple of years as a salesperson in the computer department of an electronics store. When I was hired, my boss explained that my job wasn't just to help people find the right computer; it was to help maximize the store's profits by recommending accessories and other items to go with their purchase. The job was all about "upselling"—what fast-food restaurants do when they ask if you want to make that a combo and what online booksellers do when they tell you which books other people like you are reading.

As I watched the other salespeople in my department, I noticed that they could be roughly divided into three groups. In one group were the passive salespeople. They stood around idly waiting for a customer to approach them, and once a customer had decided what to buy, they would sell that customer exactly what he or she asked for—no more, no less. These salespeople were generally liked by the customers who wanted a quick transaction, but they didn't have very good sales numbers because they didn't upsell. The customer left with only the things they already knew they wanted from the start.

In the second group were the aggressive salespeople. They were determined to upsell at all costs, and they usually had their favorite things to recommend to every customer. They'd pressure every customer into buying the same extended warranty package, for instance, just because it was a profitable item for the store. If the customer didn't want it, they'd just keep pressuring and pressuring until the customer either gave in or got too upset to continue. These employees tended to have high sales numbers on paper, but customers hated dealing with them. On occasion, I saw a customer leave the store in tears because of this group's high-pressure sales tactics.

But the best salespeople were in the third group. They did one important thing that neither of the other groups did: *They listened.* In a friendly, nonthreatening way, they'd ask every customer a bit about what they wanted out of their purchase, and they'd tailor their behavior and recommendations to the customer's needs and wants. With the busy business executive, they'd process the sale quickly. With the overwhelmed grandmother, they'd take their time explaining things. Instead of trying to sell everyone the same add-on item, they'd use what they'd heard to offer a custom solution:

> "You said you just got a digital camera for Christmas? We have a sale on high-quality photo paper and ink this week; may I show you where it is?"

"Here's some educational software your daughter
might like as she's learning to use her first computer."
"Since you play a lot of computer games, you could
benefit from this new graphics card we just got in."

These were the salespeople whose customers returned over
and over again, asking for them by name. This group helped
maximize the store's profits, yes, but at the same time, they helped
meet their customers' needs. They created a win-win situation
where everyone ended up happy. And they did it by listening to
their customers and treating every person as an individual, not
trying to fit them into some one-size-fits-all memorized routine.

Before that job, I'd always thought of salespeople as shady
characters—the sort who would tell you anything just to get more
of your cash. Some salespeople are like that. But in that job, I
learned that the best way to sell someone on something—whether
it's a computer or an idea—is to listen to them, pay attention to
what they really want and care about, and then find a win-win
scenario. It's not about tricking them into something they don't
want; it's about finding that sweet spot where you're both happy.

If you can learn to do that, you can accomplish great things
in the world. And the key is strategic listening.

What Is Strategic Listening?

"Strategic listening" is an information-gathering process to help you find the most effective ways to reach someone with a new idea or a different perspective of the world. It's exactly what it sounds like: listening carefully while someone else talks, and paying attention to what you can learn from what they have to say. For example:

- **What do they want?** What are their motivations and priorities? What's important to them about this issue? They may have deeper interests driving their disagreement.
- **What do they believe?** How deep is their understanding of this issue? What misconceptions do they have? There may be areas in which you need to educate them.
- **What do they think *you* want?** How well do they understand your priorities? What do they think you're all about? Their image of you might be very different from your image of yourself.
- **What are their sources of information?** What authorities, news sources, etc., do they trust? Citing sources they trust will get you further than citing ones they distrust.

- **What language do they use?** Do they use certain phrases or terminology that you're unfamiliar with or that stand out as unique to their bubble? These are clues to their influences.
- **What are they worried about?** Fear is a particularly strong motivator. Take extra note of any expressions of concern about the future.
- **What do you have in common?** Whether it's a shared background or a shared concern, common ground helps you humanize each other and provides a great starting point for future conversation.

Whenever possible, this kind of listening should be the very first thing you do after establishing expectations for your strategic dialogue. *Always listen to them first before asking them to listen to you.* And as you listen, go out of your way to be inquisitive, sensitive, and sincere.

Always listen to them first before asking them to listen to you.

Be inquisitive.

Don't just sit quietly. Actively engage them with open-ended questions that encourage them to talk about themselves and their views. I like to start off my dialogues by asking the other person to tell me their story—their background, their family, how they got connected to this subject, why it matters to them, how they see the issue, why they agreed to talk to me about it. Essentially, I want to hear how they would tell the story of their involvement with this issue.

With some people, this is easy; I just have to ask them to tell me a bit about themselves, and the whole story comes tumbling out. With others, it requires asking more questions. Typically, you won't directly ask the questions just mentioned, as they're a bit blunt, but you can keep them in mind to help you think of situation-appropriate questions. Whatever you ask, though, avoid "leading" questions that might make them defensive, like, "How can you justify your view, given all the evidence against you?" Instead, keep the questions light and open, like, "You seem to be very passionate about this subject. I'd love to know more about what makes it so important to you."

Be sensitive.

Just as with the customers at the electronics store, it's important to be sensitive to the body language and responses of the person in front of you. Most people like talking about themselves and their views, but some people are very private or may not feel comfortable enough with you to open up. You don't ever want to make people feel like you're prying, so if someone doesn't seem to feel comfortable opening up about themselves, don't force it. It's still important to listen as much as you can, and if they begin opening up more later in the conversation, that's your cue to shut up and let them talk.

Be sincere.

When you listen, listen *sincerely*. Your number one goal at this point is to *understand this person as well as you possibly can*. This isn't some kind of trick or manipulation; you want to understand them, and they want to be understood. Yes, listening is strategic, but it also needs to be genuine. When I'm listening to people in these situations, I don't have to *act* interested, because I genuinely *am* interested. If I want to convince this person to think about something differently, I first need to understand what makes them tick. In the process, I often find that I come to genuinely care about people who I'd previously thought of as enemies. The more I listen to them, the easier it is for me to understand why they see the world the way they do. That doesn't mean I disagree with them any less, but it does mean that I am able to humanize them in ways I couldn't before.

Once you get the hang of it, you'll find that strategic listening is one of the most powerful techniques to break down echo chambers. But it can be difficult at first to get used to the idea of *listening* as powerful. In the middle of a conflict, especially one where we're deeply invested in the outcome, our natural instinct is to talk, not listen. We go into these conversations preparing ourselves for battle, armed with all our best arguments, ready to destroy whatever arguments they might throw back at us.

But remember, the goal of this interaction isn't just to "win" the argument. This isn't a debate tournament. You might very well have the best argument, but even if you successfully out-argue them at every point, you can't make them agree with you.

"Winning" the argument counts for nothing if the other person winds up angrily digging in their heels.

In my evangelical church growing up, we had a saying: "You can't argue someone to the Lord." This is true of any attempt to change someone's mind, whether the subject is religious, politi-

Arguments alone don't change minds.

cal, or something else entirely. *Arguments alone don't change minds.* If you want to have the best chance of bringing this other person around to your way of thinking, you have to have patience, you have to be strategic, and you have to be willing to listen.

Room-Temperature Eggs

I wish I had spent more time with my mom in the kitchen when I was young. She was an excellent cook, whereas I feel accomplished if my frozen dinner heats evenly. But I do remember watching her make one of her famous lemon meringue pies with a light, fluffy meringue that no one else seemed able to imitate.

"This," she said, pointing to the eggs on the counter, "is the secret. You have to have room-temperature eggs."

That sounded like nonsense to me. "Why room temperature?"

"It changes how they beat," she explained. "You have to take the eggs out of the refrigerator early, because room-temperature eggs make a fluffier meringue. A lot of people overlook that one simple step. They try to save time by using eggs right out of the fridge, and then they don't understand why their meringue isn't as fluffy. But it's such a simple thing: You have to be patient and let the eggs warm up to room temperature first."

The listening step of strategic dialogue is a lot like that. When you put this strategy into practice in real-world situations, you'll find yourself *really* tempted to skip over the listening step. It will seem unnecessary, especially when you feel confident that you already understand the other person's point of view or are tired of hearing them talk. You'll want to jump ahead to the next step, to the "good parts," where you get to talk. How much difference could it really make? But I promise you, if you don't take plenty of time to formally and deliberately listen to the other person, your final product won't be nearly as successful.

When you begin your conversation by *listening* instead of talking, you accomplish more than just gathering information. Right from the start, you're setting a tone of cooperation rather than antagonism. You're sending a message to the other person that they aren't going to have to fight you in order to be heard by you. If the other person is coming into the conversation with anger or fear or stress, you're giving them the opportunity to get that off their chest right away.

Being listened to tends to calm people down. My friend Michael once told me that during his training for a customer service job, his company taught him to never tell an angry customer, "Calm down." Instead, he was encouraged to listen and show sympathy. This is excellent advice. No angry person ever wants to be *told* to calm down—that just feels belittling. Most of the time, what they really want is to be heard, to know that someone else cares about the thing that's upsetting them.

Listening to someone also makes it more likely that they'll ultimately be willing to listen to you. Without making a big deal about it, you're modeling for them how this conversation should go. If you're quick to interrupt and argue with them, they're more likely to do the same back. But if you listen respectfully and attentively, showing genuine interest and asking questions, they're more likely to do the same.

A couples' therapist I know gives a listening exercise to his clients with communication issues: One partner has to remain quiet while the other partner says everything on their mind that they've had bottled up, talking for as long as they possibly can. Eventually, the speaking partner finds that they've gotten everything out that they needed to say, and there's nothing left for them to do but listen in return. Sometimes, that takes multiple rounds of them being heard, but in general, the more that people feel heard, the more likely they are to listen.

Why Don't We Listen?

So if listening is such a powerful tool, why don't we use it more often?

One reason is human nature. Even though listening is powerful, it *feels* passive. When an issue is important to us, we feel like we need to argue more fiercely, even if, in the end, that's a less effective approach.

Listening can be emotionally challenging as well; it's not always easy to stay silent while someone says things you disagree with, especially if you feel like you've already heard too much from their side and it's *your* side that isn't being heard in the conversation. If you're in the minority on an issue, staying quiet to listen to someone who has more power and influence than you feels unfair and wrong on many levels, and for good reason. You may be thinking that, by all rights, *they* should be listening to *you* first—and you may be absolutely right, but you only have the power to control your behavior, not theirs. (This is also why listening is only the first step; the strategy must ultimately continue beyond this point to be effective.)

Sometimes, people worry that taking time to listen to their opposition will delay other necessary forms of action. But remember, strategic dialogue isn't a *replacement* for appropriate political or social work to bring about change; it's a *complement* to those things. If someone is actively doing harm to people and you have the ability to take action to make them stop, by all means, take that action. Don't put it on hold for the sake of a conversation.

But taking action shouldn't preclude strategic listening, either. Understanding your opponent's motivations can help

Understanding your opponent's motivations can help you fine-tune your action plan.

you fine-tune your action plan to be even more impactful, and breaking down echo chambers can create permanent attitude change that helps your reforms stick. Without the attitude change that comes from strategic dialogue, any rule or law you put in place today could be overturned by someone else tomorrow. Like a hostage negotiator working with a police tactical team, listening and action shouldn't be either/or—they should be both/and.

One final concern is that listening to someone may feel like you're legitimizing their point of view. But *listening is not legitimizing*. Trying to understand someone doesn't mean you think they might be right. In fact, the more important it is to change someone's mind, the more critical the listening step becomes.*

Breaking Through the Barriers

Strategic listening is one of two core skills that can dramatically increase the effectiveness of your dialogue. We'll look at the other one, strategic storytelling, in a later chapter. But first, let's look at how something as simple as strategic listening can break down one of the most powerful barriers to communication on divisive issues.

*Keep in mind, the kind of listening we're talking about is *private* listening—it's part of your strategic dialogue, not giving them a public platform. If you're trying to understand someone who holds racist beliefs, for example, you absolutely do not want to have some kind of public forum that might seem to legitimize racism in the name of dialogue. There *are* circumstances where a public conversation between different points of view can be helpful, but that is a separate tactic from the strategic listening in this chapter.

The First Barrier

Ego Protection

CHAPTER 6

The Villain's Side of the Story

Are people born wicked? Or do they have wickedness thrust
upon them? After all, she had a childhood. She had a
father. . . . And she had a mother, as so many do.
—Glinda, *Wicked*[16]

_____

Well, you tried.

You sat down with Uncle John to talk about the issues on which you disagree. You were determined to listen, to be gracious, to help him see things your way—but somehow, it all went off the rails.

He started getting defensive. When you made a good point he couldn't refute, he told you that you didn't know what you were talking about and switched to another line of defense. You got frustrated when he wouldn't stick to the facts. He kept jumping around from one argument to another, like a game of Whac-A-Mole. You got angry. He got angry. You both raised your voices and said hurtful things. And now you're more convinced than ever that this man is simply impossible.

What went wrong?

You've just encountered the first of five barriers to dialogue that pop up over and over again in these kinds of situations. In this case, you've run into the *ego-protection* barrier.

The ego-protection barrier can be easily summed up in a few simple sentences:

Nobody wants to look foolish.

Nobody wants to be wrong.

Nobody wants to feel manipulated.

This is all very reasonable. But unfortunately, when you sit down with Uncle John to try to change his mind, even if you're nice about it, what he hears is, "You're foolish. You're wrong. Believe what I tell you to believe."

However much you try to sugarcoat it, that's a message most people don't want to accept. But Uncle John knows he has another option—he can assume that he's right and *you're* the one who's foolish and wrong. Guess which one sounds more appealing.

When I say that Uncle John wants to protect his "ego," I don't mean "ego" in a negative sense, like arrogance—although Uncle John might well be arrogant. I'm talking about his sense of self, his confidence and dignity. Ego protection is a kind of self-defense; he doesn't want to be humiliated.

We're all susceptible to this, not just Uncle John. Have you ever been in the middle of an argument, when the other person made a good point but you couldn't bring yourself to admit that they might be right because you were afraid of looking foolish? If so, then you've experienced the ego-protection barrier firsthand.

I've witnessed—and sometimes participated in—a number of arguments that went something like this:

Person A is angry. "I can't believe you stood me up like that! You knew I was waiting for you, and you never even bothered to call!"

But Person B has an explanation. "I *didn't* know! Check your phone. I never got your message!"

Person A can't dispute that, but they're still angry, so they shift focus. "Well, it's not even about that anyway! It's— This is how you always are!"

See what happened there? If they were being perfectly logical, Person A would have stopped the argument and apologized the minute they realized their understanding was wrong. ("You never got the message? Oh! My mistake. I'm sorry for my assumption.") But in the heat of anger, they don't want to look foolish, so they try to justify themselves by bringing up some other unresolved issue even though it wasn't really the thing that set them off to begin with.

Any time you tell someone they're wrong about something— especially if it's something they've already made a big deal about— it's going to trigger their defensive ego-protection instinct.

And, especially when we're frustrated, it's all too easy for us to approach them in a way that can cause them to dig in their heels even more. Much of the time, we go into these disagreements with an image of our opponents that isn't particularly flattering. At best, we imagine them as ignorant or stupid, having fallen for foolish beliefs being peddled by the other side. At worst, we imagine them as downright villainous, bad guys standing in the way of what's right for their own selfish reasons.

As soon as they get a whiff of that attitude from our side, they shut down immediately to protect their own sense of self.

"I'm not the ignorant one; you're the ignorant one."

"I'm not the bad guy; you're the bad guy."

An us-vs.-them mentality takes over, and as far as they're concerned, you're on the wrong side. Nothing you say can convince them otherwise, and you start to feel like you've run into a brick wall.

Sound familiar?

Thankfully, there's hope. You *can* break through the ego-protection barrier. But you can't do it with a narrative that portrays them as a villain. You're going to need a new narrative, one they will be willing to accept and work with. And that means you're going to have to do some strategic listening and hear *the villain's side of the story*.

What Makes a Villain a Villain?

In most popular movies and TV shows, it's not hard to figure out who the villain is. In children's cartoons, they twirl their mustaches and laugh maniacally. In action films, they overconfidently dare the hero to stop them as they enact elaborate plots to detonate a bomb or kill another character. From Cruella De Vil to Voldemort, classic villains tend to follow certain tropes. There's no question that they're evil, and often, even *they* seem to be aware that they're the villains.

This is all code to tell us, the audience, who we should be rooting against. It lets us shut off our brains, sit back, and be entertained without having to wrestle with questions of moral ambiguity. Sometimes, we just want to watch the hero vanquish the villain—to have a character we can unite in despising. When, at the end, the villain is caught or humiliated or killed, we delight in the schadenfreude.

In most cases, we're not expected to identify with the villain or ask probing questions about their deeper motivations. We're simply told, "She's greedy," or "He wants to take over the world," and we accept that as all the motivation needed to explain the character. The Wicked Queen in *Snow White* is, apparently, so vain that she's willing to kill anyone prettier than she is—but we don't ever stop to ask if that's reasonable or what's happened in her life to cause her to become so obsessed. She's the villain—we don't expect her to be rational, so we don't try to understand her.

But what if we did try to understand the villain? What might we learn? How would it change our view of the story?

The Broadway smash musical *Wicked* is my favorite example of this kind of storytelling. Loosely based on Gregory Maguire's novel, Broadway's version is a retelling of the story of *The Wizard of Oz* from the perspective of the Wicked Witch of the West. As *Wicked* tells it, the Wicked Witch's real name is Elphaba, a girl born with green skin and ostracized for her looks who uncovers corruption in Oz and becomes an activist to fight for what she believes in. In this version of the tale, Dorothy is only a pawn in something she doesn't fully understand, and

Dorothy's journey—culminating in her melting of the Witch with a bucket of water—is all part of a larger, more complex plot she's wholly unaware of.

In some villain-as-protagonist retellings, such as Disney's film *Maleficent*, we're told that the story we already know has the facts all wrong. But I really love the approach of *Wicked*, which tells us that the *Oz* story we know is largely true; it's just incomplete. As we grow to understand more of Elphaba's backstory, her actions throughout the classic *Oz* narrative gain new significance. *Wicked* doesn't excuse all her actions, but it does explain them, and by the end she seems far more sympathetic than the characters cheering her death.

Real-life villains are rarely as one-dimensional as they are in the movies. In real life, there's always another side—another version of events.

In the movies, the villains know they're the villains. In real life, everyone is the protagonist of their own story. The people we see as villains don't see themselves that way. They may even think *we're* the villains.

The people we see as villains don't see themselves that way.

If we approach real-life situations as if they were movie plots, we can easily fall for the intellectual laziness of thinking that our opponents are just the "bad guys" and that's all there is to it. But if we want to convince our opponents to change their minds, we need to learn to see them as they see themselves—to understand the story as they'd tell it, in a world where *they* are the protagonists.

We need a narrative with some *nuance*.

Tips for Finding a Nuanced Narrative

Humanize your opponent.

No matter how angry or frustrated you may be with Uncle John, he's not a cartoon villain. He's a complex human being with his own version of the story. Still, humanizing our opponents is hard to do. If we're honest, sometimes we're so angry and frustrated with them that we don't even *want* to see their side of things. It doesn't seem fair that *we* should have to see *their* side; we want *them* to see *our* side!

But strategic dialogue isn't always about what's fair. It's about what's effective. And the reality is that if you talk to someone as if they're a villain, you're not going to win them over. You'll trigger their ego-protection reflex, and they'll immediately discount everything you have to say. Treating someone like a villain is a great way to start a fight or provoke a war, but it's a terrible way to get people to listen to you.

If you want to win someone over, you have to fight your instinct to villainize them. Instead, work to humanize and understand them. This doesn't mean you abandon your position on the issues. You can still firmly believe that they're wrong and that their actions are harmful, but you need to do more than caricature them as one-dimensional movie villains. You need to start asking deeper questions: What motivates them? Why do they do what they do? What do they believe, and why do they believe it?

Listen for their motivations.

This is where strategic listening comes in. Right from the beginning, ask them to tell you their story—the story of what matters to them, their experience with the issue at hand, and the events that led them to the position they now hold. Listen carefully. Ask encouraging questions. Don't interrupt or argue. And as they talk, pay close attention not just to their *position* on the issue but to their *motivations*. Why is this so important to them? Answering that question is key to understanding their side of the story.

In their classic negotiation book *Getting to Yes*, authors Roger Fisher, William Ury, and Bruce Patton cite an illustration from management guru Mary Parker Follett:

> Consider [the] story of two men quarreling in a library. One wants the window open and the other wants it closed. They bicker back and forth about how much to leave it open: a crack, halfway, three-quarters of the way. No solution satisfies them both.
>
> Enter the librarian. She asks one why he wants the window open: "To get some fresh air." She asks the other why he wants it closed: "To avoid the draft." After think-

ing a minute, she opens wide a window in the next room, bringing in fresh air without a draft.[17]

This has become a classic example of the need to, as the authors put it, "focus on interests, not positions." As you listen to someone share their story, it's important to hear more than just their position on the issue at hand. Listen for their underlying wants, needs, values, concerns, and priorities—the *interests* that are motivating their *positions*. In other words, the question isn't just "What do they want?" but rather "*Why* do they want it?" This is what your response ultimately has to address.

> The question isn't just "What do they want?" but rather "*Why* do they want it?"

In the imaginary example about the window, learning each side's motivations is as simple as asking "why" one time. In real life, figuring out what someone's interests are isn't always so easy. People may give you all sorts of "reasons" for their position that only scratch the surface of what's *really* bothering them. It's important to dig deep, asking questions and listening carefully like a good journalist or therapist until you're sure you've uncovered the other person's real interests.

Don't settle for straw men.

And be very careful: It's tempting to think you already *know* what's motivating a person, and you may settle too quickly for a one-dimensional-villain answer that puts the other side in a bad light and allows you to look down on them. ("Oh, I know why he wants the window open. He wants it open because he's a selfish jerk, and he enjoys watching me scramble for my papers every time the draft blows them off my desk.")

You know, maybe that guy *is* a selfish jerk, but that's certainly not what *he* thinks of himself. And if you want to convince him to stop opening that window, it's important to know what *he* thinks his motivations are.

A few months after Donald Trump was elected president of the United States, a progressive friend of mine was complaining that he couldn't talk to his mom about politics because they were so far apart philosophically. He had voted for Clinton, she had voted for Trump, and he was angry with her for her vote.

"Do you happen to know why she voted for Trump?" I asked.

"Yes," he said. "Because she's ensconced in her cultural whiteness."

"Let me rephrase," I said. "Do you know why *she* would say she voted for Trump? Because I'm pretty sure she wouldn't say it's because she's ensconced in cultural whiteness."

He laughed.

But it's true. Imagine for a moment that you're his mom. How swayed would you be by the political argument of someone who thinks your motivation is simply that you're "ensconced in cultural whiteness"? Would you feel understood and respected? Whether his analysis of her is true or not, it's almost surely not her analysis of *herself*.

It's easy to decide that the other side's real motivation on an issue is prejudice or selfishness or greed. And sometimes, unflattering descriptions may in fact be true. Unabashed racism or sexism or selfishness or cruelty may in fact be someone's primary motivator. But unless they see *themselves* as unabashedly racist or sexist or selfish or cruel, there's still an unanswered question, the question of what *they* think their motivations are. There's nearly always more to the story.

Explain; don't excuse.

"But wait!" you may be saying. "Suppose someone really is just selfish or bigoted. Are you saying we're supposed to excuse them and let them off the hook in the name of dialogue just because they don't see themselves that way?"

Absolutely not.

It's important to distinguish between *explaining* and *excusing*. Explaining why something happened is vital if you want to stop it from happening in the future. If a train derails, experts are going to do their best to determine what went wrong—they want to *explain* the wreck. The more accurately they can explain it, the better chance they have of making sure it doesn't happen again. However, by explaining it they're not lending it any kind of legitimacy or taking away from the tragedy of what happened. They're just trying to understand why it happened.

The same is true for people. It's possible that there's no *excuse* for the behavior of someone you're talking to on the other side. Okay, then. Don't excuse it. But it's still important to try to understand and *explain* why they do what they do—what they understand to be motivating their behavior—even if you completely disagree with their rationale.

Tell their story back to them.

Once you know how to explain someone's motives, you can use that to tell their story the way *they* would tell it. This is a lot like what therapists do when they say back to you what they've heard from you, but in different language. ("So what I'm hearing you say is that when your roommate leaves out dirty dishes, you feel obligated to clean them up, and that makes you feel like she's taking advantage of you.")

Famed self-improvement author Dale Carnegie said that "a person's name is to that person the sweetest and most important sound in any language."[18] In a similar vein, one of the most comforting, encouraging things a person can ever hear from you is the sound of you telling their story the way they would tell it themselves.

When someone tells your story the way you would tell it, it makes you feel heard and understood in a way few other things can. As human beings, we want to know that someone else is paying attention to what we think and feel—that our views and experiences *matter* to someone. When you try to explain yourself to someone and they just don't get it, that's frustrating. But when someone hears you so well that they can tell your story from your perspective, that's incredibly satisfying.

When I do this, I try never to make it sound like a therapist, though. I'll say something like, "I want to make sure I really understand where you're coming from. Can you tell me if I've got this right?" And then I'll tell their story as well as I can, from their perspective, as if they were the hero of a story I was writing and I wanted that hero's every move to seem reasonable and sympathetic to the audience.

If the other person stops me and says that I've gotten something wrong, I apologize and ask them to explain that part in more depth—and then I try again. And I keep trying until the other person affirms that yes, I've understood their story from their perspective.

Remember, everyone is the protagonist of their own story. People almost never tell their own story in a way that makes them look like a villain. Even if they admit that they made bad decisions along the way, they'll still usually try to explain why they made those bad decisions—what was motivating them—so that the listener can empathize with what they've been through. If you can tell the story like that, with them as the protagonist, it transforms your entire interaction with them. You're no longer the accuser who must be defended against. You're now a friend who understands them. And that breaks down a lot of walls.

> **Remember, everyone is the protagonist of their own story.**

Know your limits—but don't be hasty.

There are always at least two sides to any conflict. Even the most despicable villain has their own version of events. That said, there are times when someone's position is so extreme or harmful that you might make a decision not to engage with them, even in private. For instance, I don't try to dialogue with people who openly spew hatred or unapologetic racism, such as white supremacists.

Of course, there's always a trade-off. Choosing not to engage with someone means you have a zero percent chance of having an impact on that person's attitudes and beliefs. Even if you don't think they would have listened to you, any chance is usually still better than no chance.

There's a fine line here. If we never engage with people we find it difficult to talk to, we only contribute to the polarization problem. Fighting polarization requires listening to the apparent "villains" even when you don't want to. But that doesn't mean you have to sit down with the KKK. Sometimes you have to draw a line, and it's up to you to decide where your own line is.

A few years ago, I had an encounter with Westboro Baptist Church, a hate group that travels around the US with offensive, inflammatory signs about all the people they claim God "hates." They're most famous for saying "God hates fags," but they also target many other groups. They've picketed schools, churches, funerals, and sites of tragedies. They make all sorts of outrageous and upsetting statements—thanking God for events like the Boston Marathon bombing, telling mourning families of soldiers and hate-crime victims that their loved ones are in hell, and using vile language to describe anyone they disagree with. Although they are not physically violent, they have caused a tremendous amount of pain to many people. Frustratingly, they get a lot of press, and they seem to know exactly how far they can push things and stay within the law, making it difficult to do anything about them.

In many ways, Westboro is the perfect counterexample to a chapter about listening to your opponents. No amount of listening (and no amount of arguing) is going to convince this group to change their minds. If you ever happen to be someplace where Westboro is protesting, I don't recommend engaging with them at all.

And yet, even here, there are ways strategic listening has power.

My friend Jeff Chu is a journalist who also happens to be both gay and Christian. He's very skilled in the art of listening, and he knows just how to ask questions that invite people to open up about their passions. I first met Jeff when he was conducting interviews for his excellent book, *Does Jesus Really Love Me?*, which tells the story of his journeys across the country to meet folks on all sides of the Christian conversation about sexual orientation.[19] It's a compelling read, but one chapter is particularly compelling— and horrifying. Jeff, a soft-spoken, slightly built gay man, decided to go do some listening at *Westboro Baptist Church*.

I've built my whole career on talking to people who disagree with me, especially on issues of faith and sexuality, and even I don't have the guts to go to Westboro. I truly don't know how Jeff did it. But he did, and the conversations that resulted are fascinating to read.

What Jeff came to understand was that the members of the Westboro clan are essentially extreme Calvinists. They believe that God has predestined certain people to be saved, regardless of anything anyone does. Unlike Evangelicals, who try to preach persuasive messages to convince people to make a *decision* to be saved, Westboro has no interest in being persuasive because they don't think it matters. They believe it's already predestined. Instead of being persuasive, they simply want to be *heard*—for everyone to *know* that God's wrath is coming so that they have "no excuse" when the time comes.

It's a dark, twisted theology, but once you understand this about them, a lot of other things about their behavior makes sense. Their offensive signs and slogans were never designed to change anyone's mind; they were designed, instead, to shock people and get media attention. Their choice of high-profile targets and controversial tactics, and their strategy of notifying local media in advance of their arrival, are all deliberate attempts to stir up anger and thus get more attention. The counter-protests they often inspire, which in turn draw more media, don't bother them one bit. Indeed, it's exactly what they want.

Not long after Jeff shared the story of his journey with me, I received some very unwelcome news: Westboro was coming to protest a conference my organization was running. In typical fashion, they'd announced their plans days in advance, and as the guy in charge, I had to figure out how we would respond.

I knew that many of the attendees at this particular conference were at difficult points in their lives: conservative parents whose children had just come out to them, LGBT Christians struggling to accept themselves, and countless other people who had dealt with hard times over the preceding year. The last thing these folks needed was a group of protestors shouting at them.

I discussed the situation with our leadership and shared with them what I had learned from Jeff. Our response, organized by our board chair in collaboration with members of the local community, was partly inspired by what Jeff's listening had taught us.

Westboro was set to protest us on a Saturday morning, just before the first session of the day. The conference was being held in a convention center, but most of the attendees were staying at a hotel a block away. Westboro was going to be standing in a spot between the two buildings, ensuring that all our attendees would have to walk right past the protestors on their way to the convention center.

That morning, a large group of parents and local church members got up early. They brought signs with loving messages on them, gathered in front of the convention center, and then stood shoulder to shoulder along the street with their backs to the protestors, facing the path the conference attendees would travel. They began singing songs to drown out the protestors and waited for the conference attendees to arrive.

As people made their way from the hotel to the convention center that morning, they were greeted by a kind of human path directly into the building, with cheerful songs, friendly faces, encouraging signs, and words of welcome. Instead of arguing with the protestors or doing anything to generate media attention, the anti-protestors had quietly organized a way to block them from view and ensure that conference attendees would hear messages of love, not hate.

It rained that morning, on protestors and supporters alike. But the parents and local church members kept smiling, greeting people, and singing songs, as—I kid you not—a big, beautiful rainbow appeared over the whole scene.

The protestors went home early. Many people never even saw them.

Even with a hate group, there are ways that listening can help you develop a strategic response. But, with that said, as grateful as I am for Jeff's willingness to help me understand Westboro and develop a plan to combat them, I'm not advocating sitting down with hate groups to listen to their hate.

So, yes, I'd say there are exceptions. But be careful before you write someone off. We were able to gain something by listening even to Westboro Baptist Church, and if half the country seems as unreachable to you as Westboro, you may need to recalibrate your basis for measurement.

Expect the unexpected.

If ego protection were the only major barrier, you could stop reading right here and have a great strategy for changing hearts and minds. But people are a little more complicated than that. As you work to break through Uncle John's ego-protection barrier, you'll probably find other barriers popping up in ways you hadn't expected. That's okay. Keep listening and making mental notes of what you hear. There are ways to get through those other barriers as well. In the next chapter, we'll look at a particularly challenging one that is tearing our country apart.

The Second Barrier

Team Loyalty

CHAPTER 7

Challenging Us-vs.-Them Mindsets

She wanted to be able to label me, to put me on a shelf. This
is what most people want, because focusing on labels makes
life easier. Label yourself and you'll always know what to
think, even without thinking; label others and you'll always
know who are your enemies and who are your friends.

—Bruce Bawer[20]

"I hope it fails."

You're on a coffee break, reading something on your phone, when your co-worker Michelle breaks the silence with these words. You glance up.

"Sorry," you say. "I wasn't listening. You hope *what* fails?"

"That bill they're trying to push through," she says, gesturing to a local news story playing on a muted TV. "I hope it fails and teaches them a lesson."

The bill in question is something being debated by your local legislature. It's an attempt to modernize your industry in a way that would broadly benefit the community, but partisan arguments about the details keep stalling the progress.

You and Michelle belong to different political parties, but

you've always gotten along. Now, though, you're confused: the proposed bill seems like something *both* parties should be able to agree on. Two years earlier, when Michelle's party had a majority, they tried to get a similar bill passed. It didn't get enough votes, but at the time, Michelle was very much in favor of it. Now, your party has a majority, and they've proposed a bill very similar to the one from two years earlier, with a new name and some minor changes to make it seem like something different. Still, it's basically the same thing Michelle supported at the time. So why is she now so against it?

"It's not the same at all," she says when you ask her. "And if they liked the idea, they should have supported it the first time around."

"Well," you reply, "there were some issues that needed to be addressed with the earlier version—"

"That's bull," she snaps back. "They just wanted credit. This is the kind of thing your party does all the time. They want to look good, and they don't care who they hurt in the process."

"What are you talking about? *Your* party is the one playing politics with this bill."

The fight continues.

The bill dies in committee.

You don't get invited to Michelle's next barbecue.

And you can't help thinking to yourself, if it's this hard to get people to work together when they want the same thing, how can we hope to build understanding on issues on which we genuinely disagree?

The Second Barrier

Team loyalty is a massive hurdle for any cross-divide dialogue. In our polarized society, people tend to see the world in terms of opposing teams, defined by whatever they see as important—politics, religion, social circles, etc. They trust the information and opinions of people on their "team," and they mistrust the information and opinions of their opponents' teams.

The minute people associate you with *the other side*—a different political party, for instance—many will automatically write off everything you say. ("Just what I'd expect from a clueless liberal!" "Typical male Republican.") You might get told that you're "biased" and can't be objective on a subject because of your membership in a particular cultural group—with the implication that only *the other side* can be objective. Or they might hold you responsible for the words or actions of other members of your group, even though you have very little in common with those individuals. ("You people are such hypocrites. Just look at [some person you've never met].")

Any time you hear this kind of language, you know that—at least for the other person—this conflict is about more than the two of you. They see this as a battle between different teams—Republicans vs. Democrats, gays vs. Christians, Apple vs. Android—and as far as they're concerned, you're not trustworthy, because you're on the wrong team.

The Surprising Power of Teams

A lot of us are in denial about how much our political, social, and other "teams" affect our thinking. But they really do have a major influence on us—and on the people whose minds we want to change.

In a series of experiments at Yale, subjects were given the details of two welfare policy proposals and asked to evaluate them. Conservative Republicans favored "stringent" welfare plans, and liberal Democrats favored "generous" ones. No surprise there. But if subjects were told that their party had taken a stand for or against a given proposal, *people claimed their party's supposed position as their own, no matter which position that was*:

> Regardless of whether the policy was generous or stringent, liberal participants supported it if told that Democrats supported it . . . and they opposed it if told Democrats opposed it. . . . Likewise, conservative participants supported the policy if told that Republicans supported it . . . and they opposed it if told Republicans opposed it. . . . By contrast, policy content had no direct effect for either partisan group.[21]

On both sides of the aisle, people were so committed to their political "team" that they just went with whatever they believed their party liked—even if, in other circumstances, it would have contradicted their own personal judgment. This was true no matter how much knowledge the participants had about welfare beforehand. Team loyalty outweighed everything else.

Conservatives took positions advocating for a welfare policy *more generous than any real-world policy*, and liberals took positions advocating for a welfare policy *more stringent than any real-world policy*—just because they were told that this was the position of others in their party. This was even true when the two policies were detailed side by side, allowing subjects to see for themselves how a policy compared to its alternative.

It's easy for us to sit and smugly shake our heads at the subjects of these experiments. *They* might be so easily swayed by team loyalty, we think, but *we* surely wouldn't fall for that! *We* know why we believe what we do, and it's definitely not just because of what our parties tell us, right? Well, guess what: The experimental subjects thought the same thing. When asked which factors had influenced their position, they were sure it was a result of their own analysis, not their party's position—even though they recognized that party politics had an influence on *other* people:

> Participants thus asserted that they had based their attitude on an autonomous and rational consideration of the facts . . . but they ascribed the beliefs of their allies, and especially those of their adversaries, to group influence.[22]

In one version of the experiment, people even wrote detailed editorials explaining the rationale behind their position—making a passionate case that this was the logical position, unaware the view they were now so passionate about had been directly manipulated by the researcher.

This is how we all tend to think. We know that other people's beliefs—especially our opponents' beliefs—are influenced by their echo chambers, but we think our own beliefs are rational and objective, unaware of the influence of our own teams. This is important to understand, because it means our opponents think the same thing; they assume we're just a product of our echo chambers and that *they're* the ones thinking rationally.

Amazingly, this us-vs.-them approach to the world can happen even when the choice of "teams" is purely arbitrary. When schoolteacher Jane Elliott famously divided her class into two groups based on eye color as part of a lesson on racism, the students internalized the difference and began to treat one another poorly.[23] When psychologist Muzafer Sherif randomly assigned boys to two separate groups and had them compete with each other, each group's members began describing their own group in glowing terms and the other group in negative ones—with tensions eventually rising to the point that a portion of the study had to be ended early.[24] In short, we assume the best in our own team and the worst in other teams.

Team loyalty can even change what we believe the objective facts are. In one study, students from Princeton and Dartmouth watched footage of a football game between their two schools and attempted to objectively count the number of rules infractions made by each team. But however objective they thought they were being, they couldn't escape their own biases: Princeton students counted twice as many infractions by Dartmouth players as Dartmouth students counted.[25]

Fighting the Team-Loyalty Barrier

Team loyalty seems to be baked into our humanity. We all do it, and we do it without thinking. In a game of football, that's not such a bad thing. But if we're talking about issues that matter, it can be a problem. Our loyalties can alter our perceptions, blind us to the facts, and affect our judgment in ways we don't realize.

So what can we do about it?

Get outside your own bubble.

Team loyalty doesn't just influence those people out there. It influences *all* of us. As our world becomes increasingly polarized, it's easier than ever for us to segregate ourselves into groups of people whom we perceive to be "like us"—leaving us just as susceptible to echo chambers and groupthink as the folks we disagree with. So before we can effectively fight team loyalty on their side, we need to fight it in ourselves.

In your life, look for opportunities to get outside your own bubble and listen to what other groups are saying. There are lots of ways to do this:

- Spend time with groups of people you disagree with. Hang out with friends, schoolmates, or co-workers whose teams are different from yours. Don't force them to explain themselves to you, but do pay attention to ways their views and experiences are different from yours.
- Actively work to maintain diverse connections on social media. Engage (but don't argue or debate) with posts from perspectives that are different from your own.
- Search for interesting bloggers, vloggers, and authors who write or speak about issues from other perspectives. Read or watch them regularly and pay attention to recurring themes in their work.
- When you struggle to understand the views of a friend or acquaintance, check out who they follow on social media or ask for recommendations of books or websites to help you understand their perspective.
- When a controversial issue is in the news and the right answer seems obvious to you, go out of your way to look for columns, articles, and analysis that support the other side. See if you can figure out what's driving the disagreement.

But beware: As you listen to those outside your bubble, it can be tempting to focus on only the loudest or most extreme voices on the other side—those who have made their name by pushing the envelope and stirring the pot. If you can listen to them without getting angry, it can certainly be instructive—they do have a following, after all—but it's important not to focus all your energy on the extremists who are easiest for you to dismiss. Instead, pay attention to the most reasonable, moderate voices on the other side. Take the time to try to understand their logic, their concerns, and their interests.

These outside viewpoints can help you keep your own team loyalty in check, and ultimately, they can give you insight to help you pop others' bubbles as well. As difficult as it may be to spend time outside your bubble, the perspective you gain from learning how other teams see things can end up being one of your most valuable assets as you work to change hearts and minds. With that perspective, you're much better equipped to recognize and fight the team-loyalty barrier in others.

Talk about your individuality.

Getting outside your bubble can help with your own polarized thinking, but what about others'? Let's say you're in the middle of a dialogue when you start to realize that the other person is operating out of an us-vs.-them mindset—they're a Montague, and you're a Capulet. They don't trust your Capulet news sources or your Capulet friends, and you're beginning to wonder how you'll ever have any kind of productive conversation when they seem to object to your very existence as a Capulet.

One way to push past the team-loyalty barrier is to focus on who you and the other person are as individuals, separate from your teams. You're not a Capulet having a conversation with a Montague—you're just Carol having a conversation with Mike.

This is the simplest route, and it's the easiest to use in situations where the team-loyalty barrier isn't that strong.

If you're taking this approach, you might try to avoid any references to your respective teams altogether, or you might try to point out ways in which you are different from the stereotypes about your team. If the other person brings up their team, you might try to get them to talk about times they've disagreed with the majority opinion of their team or ways they're different from most people on their team. This is a subtle way of reinforcing that the teams aren't always right and that sometimes it's necessary to go against the team grain and think as an individual.

Sometimes, you'll find that the other person *already* doesn't see you as a "real" part of your team. And while that can be helpful in getting past the team-loyalty barrier, it can also cause some problems in the long run.

When I first came out to my parents, for instance, they were absolutely convinced that I *wasn't* gay, because they couldn't reconcile their positive view of me with their negative view of gay people.

"Maybe you just haven't met the right girl yet."

"Did kids make fun of you and call you gay at school?"

"Just because you're more into academics than sports doesn't mean you're gay, you know."

For my parents, "gay people" were a monolithic group that had nothing to do with us. We were Christians; they were gays—

two separate groups with opposing cultural agendas and absolutely nothing in common.

Even once my parents did finally start to accept that I was gay, they still found ways to keep me separate from the monolithic gay "team" in their minds: They envisioned me as the *exception*.

"You're not like them," they said. "You're different." This allowed them to continue to love and support me as their beloved son without changing their negative views of the gay community. But it also made it very difficult for me to talk to them about issues affecting gay people. I could suggest books or share things I'd learned, but if they viewed the information as coming from the gay "team," they quickly dismissed it as unreliable. In their minds, gay people were still the opponents, and anything that seemed "too gay" was therefore coming from a contaminated source.

It can sometimes be useful to gain a reputation as "one of the good ones"—the "one decent conservative" or the "one reasonable feminist." It allows you to be heard in a way that others in your group might not be. But there are limits to being the "good one," especially if part of your goal is to change their attitude toward the rest of your group.

It all depends on what you're trying to accomplish. If your goal isn't really about your group, then maybe it's fine for them to completely separate you from the group in their mind. For instance, if you're liberal and trying to get a conservative friend to support your position on climate change, it's probably a big advantage if they don't see you as a typical liberal.

On the other hand, if you're an African American man who wants to combat stereotypes of African American men, it doesn't help you if people separate you out as "one of the good ones." That just allows them to continue being prejudiced against other people.

In cases like that, separating yourself from your team can backfire, and you may find that other strategies are more effective.

Redraw the team lines.

Rather than simply distancing yourself from the teams, a more powerful (though slightly more challenging) strategy is to redefine the "team" lines *so that you're both on the same team.*

For example, when I talk to Evangelicals about my experiences as a gay man in the church, I don't ignore the influence of our groups. Instead, I focus on the group influence we have in common. I speak to them as a fellow Evangelical who understands the importance and challenges of our shared faith. In this sense, we're not on different teams at all. We're on the *same* team.

Start by looking for common ground: What do you have in common with the other side, or at least with the person you're talking to? What sorts of things might bind the two of you together in ways that would put you on the same team rather than opposing ones?

Use any opportunity you can to find things you share. Start with points of identity that are important to this person—their faith, nationality, race, gender, membership in certain groups, etc. Do you share any of these in common with them? Talk about that. Those are teams you're on together.

Take it further: Do you have shared hardships or other shared experiences? Perhaps you've worked for the same demanding boss or have both experienced the challenges of poverty, for instance. If so, start a conversation about that, and use it as a chance to bond.

Do you have shared interests? Maybe you both love board games or scary movies. Maybe you root for the same football team or can't get enough of the same author. Talk about that, too.

Even if the only thing you have in common with this person is that you're part of the same family or live in the same part of the world, that's a point of identity. Talk about what it means to you to be an American—or what it means to be a Jones. The more things you have in common, the easier it is to combat an us-vs.-them mentality by emphasizing your points of shared identity.

When the students at my college dialogue event started talking to one another and adding one another on social media, that's part of what they were doing: They were learning things about one another that showed them how much they had in common. Suddenly, that girl across the aisle wasn't just "a member of the LGBT community"; she was "a fan of my favorite obscure TV show" and "someone who cares about the well-being of this school." And that started to change how they drew the team lines.

On some issues, you can ultimately use these points of shared identity to explain why your position on the issue at hand is supported by the values of your shared team. "As Americans, we value liberty for all, including those we disagree with, and that's why I believe . . ." "As a fellow teacher, I've seen what a difference it makes when kids aren't getting the care they need at home, and that's why it matters to me that . . ." One gay college student I know wrote a brilliant piece for his school newspaper in which he emphasized his team spirit and passion for the school while making the case that supporting LGBT students was a natural outgrowth of the school's own code of ethics. It's much more powerful when you can make a case for your view based on *shared* team identity and values rather than building your case on the values of an outsider team.

Find common "enemies."

As part of your shared team identity, you might also think about the shared "enemies" you have. What are you both against?

Throughout history, groups have used the idea of "uniting against a common enemy" to build alliances. Sadly, that "common enemy" often ends up being other groups of people, who then wind up persecuted as scapegoats. That may be effective, but I believe it's deeply immoral. Please don't do that.

Instead, I recommend choosing a nonhuman "enemy" you can join forces to fight. Join to fight ignorance or poverty or prejudice or any sort of problem your teams have in common. Make the battle against that shared enemy the thing that defines your team and enables you to draw the line in a way that puts you on the same side.

Need help thinking of a shared enemy? Keep this in mind during your strategic listening. Pay attention to what really matters to that person, and keep listening until you find a cause you can really get behind. Tell them stories of how you, too, have been impacted by the failing local economy (for instance), and ask them to say more about their thoughts on how to fix the problem. Suddenly, you're no longer on opposite sides; you're working together on a common problem.

What Happens When Team Loyalty Takes Over?

What if you do everything you can to find common ground with Michelle, but she just stays fixated on this black-and-white approach, her team against your team? How do you move forward if she just can't stand to let your team succeed?

Team loyalty is a massive problem in our polarized society. Sometimes, despite your best efforts, you may find that people's team loyalty becomes such a big deal that it overshadows everything else. In the next chapter, we'll look at one more strategy for handling those situations when it really does become all about the teams.

CHAPTER 8

When Teams Get Tense

"Are you coming to bed?"

"I can't. This is important."

"What?"

"Someone is wrong on the internet."

—Randall Munroe's *xkcd*[26]

In late 2014, more than one thousand conservative Southern Baptists gathered in Nashville for a conference on "the future of marriage." Tensions were high; it was months before the Supreme Court's *Obergefell* decision granted marriage rights to same-sex couples, but it was already clear which way the culture was headed. Polls showed ever-increasing support for same-sex marriage—not only legally but theologically as well. That was bad news for the traditional teachings of the Southern Baptist Church, which held that male-female marriage was ordained by God and that this change in the culture's views on marriage was evidence of a world moving further and further away from God's will.

I attended the conference not only as part of my strategic-dialogue work but also because this was a very personal topic for me. Having grown up Southern Baptist, I still thought of Southern Baptists as "my people." As a gay man, though, I also knew many Southern Baptists would see me as one of the bad guys, teaching and believing something sinful.

A major focus of the conference was the Southern Baptist response to a culture that no longer agreed with them, and there was a lot of conversation, both on and off the stage, about how to view the LGBT community. Some attendees and speakers expressed misconceptions about LGBT people that were so far off base they made me cringe. At the same time, I also heard some speakers offer genuine expressions of a desire to show more love to LGBT people, recognizing that the church had not always done well in this area.

But whatever nuance there might have been was quickly overshadowed by the polarization. I heard a number of people, oblivious to my presence, talking about LGBT people as the enemy—a monolithic group with a dangerous agenda. To hear them tell it, LGBT people were sick, selfish, and sex-obsessed, silencing anyone who disagreed with their hedonistic lives. Two speakers talked about LGBT people with such venom that I almost had to leave the room, and when they received thunderous applause, I felt sick to my stomach.

Meanwhile, a number of LGBT people and other progressive critics of the Southern Baptist Church were watching the conference via a live internet stream, tweeting their anger at what they were hearing—not just at the more divisive rhetoric but even at the attempts to express love, which they viewed as falling far short. This, naturally, did not endear them to the Southern Baptists.

One online viewer wrote that a popular speaker was "babbling nonsense. God, I may throw up."

"Is anyone really surprised by what's coming out of [this conference]?" wrote another. "Did anyone think they would be concerned about anything but themselves?"

The angry tweets from non–Southern Baptist viewers, some of them vulgar and insulting, flooded the conference's Twitter stream. For the Southern Baptists watching the stream from within the conference, it felt like an invasion from an unwelcome force that did not understand them.

One Southern Baptist supporter, responding to the flood of opposition, tweeted, "We must understand when [the] Word of God is exalted at any conference, the enemy doesn't like it, and they will resist the truth," to which someone responded, "YOUR TOTALLY FAKE Piety is shining through LOUD AND CLEAR."

The polarizing rhetoric wasn't limited to one side, but to some people, it felt like it was. "Seems there's a vast diff. in tone b/w the presenters and the critics," tweeted one pastor.

As the event ended, the Southern Baptists seemed convinced they had held a nuanced conference, standing for their theology while expressing love for those who disagreed. The online LGBT viewers, however, were convinced that the Southern Baptists were ignorant, condescending bigots. The Southern Baptists, in turn, thought the LGBT viewers had shown their toxic, intolerant nature.

In theory, each of these groups wanted to change the other's mind.

As far as I can tell, no one's mind was changed.

"This Town Ain't Big Enough . . ."

The issues that divide us are sometimes very important. I have strong opinions about who's right or wrong, and what they're right or wrong about, in the clash between the Southern Baptists and the LGBT community. You probably do, too. I believe that getting the answers right is important and has a major impact on people's lives.

But one of the things that scares me so much about our current culture of polarization is how quickly we're willing to go from "I disagree with these people" to "These people are the enemy." We talk about our neighbors as if they were wicked, irredeemable villains because of their political or social views, and we write off half the country as somehow beyond the reach of reason. We've fallen into an us-vs.-them mentality, and we're losing the ability—or even perhaps the will—to try to reach "them."

Meanwhile, they're treating us the same way, which only makes things worse. Even if we were willing to get past *our* negative view of *them* initially, knowing that *they're* treating *us* as villains makes us feel defensive. Perhaps they're even taking actions that could harm us or are already harming people we care about. We have to fight back! So we do, and the chance of understanding one another seems to wither and die amid an all-out culture war.

Imagine being at that conference as a member of one of those two groups—the Southern Baptists or the LGBT community.

Imagine trying to have a productive conversation with members of the other side in the midst of all that anger. How far do you think you'd get, once it became clear you were "one of *them*"?

If our cultural groups are so angry at each other that they can barely stand the sight of one another, how can you hope to have productive dialogue with a friend or family member who values their team loyalty above all else?

Understanding Their Team

In battling team loyalty, the most challenging strategy of all is also the most effective. When team loyalty threatens to over-shadow everything else, sometimes you need to work to *understand their team's story* just like you worked to understand their personal story.

Teams have stories just as individuals do. The Southern Baptists' story of that marriage conference is a very different story from the LGBT viewers' story of that same conference. Each of these groups sees itself as the protagonists and the other side as the villains, and each of these groups would describe the purpose and impact of that conference very differently from how the other side would.

Teams have stories just as individuals do.

These two groups' stories go much further than just the conference, though. Their conference stories are actually deeply rooted in much bigger stories of the histories these groups have with one another and with the culture at large. Each has concerns and fears and *interests* behind its *positions*. There's a reason the Southern Baptists held that conference. There's a reason the LGBT viewers watched it. For each group, this *matters*. And in a clash like this, our natural instinct is to speak up in defense of the group we agree with and dismiss the viewpoint of the group we disagree with.

But try this exercise for a moment: See if you can mentally put yourself in the shoes of the group you *disagree* with in this clash. If you don't personally identify with either of these groups, pick the group that you have the *least* sympathy for. Try to imagine being in their position. If you believed the same things they believe, how would you feel? Think about everything you know about that group and try your best to see the world from their perspective. You don't have to agree with them; just try to *understand* them.

For instance, to understand the Southern Baptists' perspective of that conference, we can't just start with the first day of the event itself. We need to consider what was happening long before that: declining membership in many Christian denominations, a cultural shift away from their traditional view of marriage, a growing sense in the culture at large that Southern Baptists' beliefs were "backward," "bigoted," and "unacceptable." What might that have made them feel? What might they have been worried about?

We need to consider, too, the values that Southern Baptists hold. Southern Baptists believe that this life is only temporary and that our eternal destination depends on accepting Jesus as Savior. If the culture moves in a direction that might be seen as undermining the trustworthiness of the Bible, what happens to belief in Jesus? What happens to people's souls? Viewed through these eyes, it's easy to understand why this was such a big deal to the Southern Baptists—this could literally be seen as a battle for the *eternal destiny of people's souls.*

Likewise, if we want to understand the LGBT viewers' perspective of that conference, we need to consider their background as well. Many LGBT people have experienced tremendous discrimination and pain at the hands of religious folks, including being fired from their jobs or disowned by their parents. They've known depression and even lost friends to suicide and self-destructive behavior because of anti-LGBT messages. For many, the legal right to get married was an important step toward a world where they could live their lives free from discrimination. And yet here was a religious group trying to stop that change from happening, even for people who didn't share their religious beliefs.

If I had to guess, I'd say that most of the LGBT people who chose to view that conference were people who feel that their lives are directly affected by what the Southern Baptists say. Perhaps their families are Southern Baptist, or they live in parts of the country where Southern Baptists have a lot of influence in public policy and cultural attitudes toward LGBT people. For them, this was *personal*. It was about their own well-being and the well-being of those they love—and as they saw it, this conference was full of people talking *about* them without involving them in the conversation.

With that background on the two groups, were you able to put yourself in the shoes of the group you most disagree with? Now imagine being asked to defend that group against people who don't like them. Imagine that you're called upon to speak on their behalf, explaining their perspective in the most sympathetic way possible. Could you make an argument on their behalf? What would you say? Do you think you could do a good job of making them sound like the protagonists?

Telling the story from an opposing team's perspective is good practice. It gets you into a mode of thinking that gives you valuable insight into other groups' motivations. And that is key to breaking through other people's team-loyalty barriers.

Telling the story from an opposing team's perspective is good practice.

As a gay Christian who grew up Southern Baptist, I have an advantage in being able to mentally put myself in these two different groups' shoes. I already have a pretty good idea of what the story looks like from each side; I've lived them both. If you generally identify with one of these groups and not the other, you don't have that same advantage, and that makes this a much harder exercise. Perhaps you have difficulty putting yourself in *either* of these groups' shoes. But even if you have no direct experience with a particular team, working to understand their story is an incredibly important part of this strategy to break down the barrier that team loyalty creates.

You don't have to agree with the team. You might even think they're completely bonkers. But you need to learn how to tell the story *the way they would tell it themselves*. And just as we saw with the ego-protection barrier, telling someone's story requires listening to them.

How Do You Listen to a Team?

Every team is made up of individuals. If you asked ten different Libertarians or ten different Mexican immigrants to tell you about what really matters to their group and why, you'd get ten different answers. Sure, there'd be some overlap, but no one person can speak for an entire group of people. It's only from the outside that groups seem monolithic.

To truly understand a team's story, you'd need to listen to a lot of different people on that team. But when you're just having a one-on-one dialogue with your friend Dot, it's really just Dot's perspective that matters most. You don't need to talk to every Roman Catholic woman in the world to understand Dot's perspective on what it means to be a Roman Catholic woman. You only need to ask Dot.

And you *should* ask Dot. As you practice strategic listening with her—or *any* time you're getting to know her—pay attention to the group identities she talks about, and ask questions about those groups. It's an important way to learn about what matters to her.

There's no single formula or script for asking about people's groups. Certainly don't treat people as if they're in an interrogation room or playing Twenty Questions. But if you need some help thinking about the sorts of things you might want to ask about, here are some of the kinds of questions I often ask people as I'm getting to know them:

"How long have you been a member of this group?"

"What is it that draws you to this group?"

"What's your sense of how the outside world views this group?"

"What do you wish more people understood about your group?"

"Are there parts of the group you disagree with or ways you feel the group doesn't represent you?"

You get the idea. As you listen and learn, try to piece together the story of how this group might tell the story with itself as the protagonist—and how the person you're talking to might tell the story of their interaction with the group.

Will the Real Victim Please Stand Up?

One more note before we leave the subject of team stories: As you listen to the other side's version of the story, you may find—to your surprise and frustration—that they see themselves as oppressed, victimized, or marginalized in a situation where you're quite sure they're not. It's not at all uncommon to have situations where *both sides* see themselves as the oppressed minority in the same conflict.

Sometimes it's easy to understand how both sides might feel victimized. Other times, it's a lot harder. A group may see themselves as somehow disadvantaged even if, from your perspective, *they're* the ones with all the power. You might look at all the advantages they have and be tempted to wonder what sort of bizarro world they're living in to think they're the disadvantaged ones. And yet they're convinced that they are.

This can happen for a lot of reasons. Sometimes both sides really do experience marginalization at the same time, just in different ways. Other times, it might be strictly in their heads. But even if the other side isn't really oppressed at all, that *feeling* of being oppressed is real to them, which means they'll behave accordingly. So if someone tells you they feel like their side is being oppressed in some way, take that seriously. It will tell you a lot about what to expect from them.

When people feel trapped or disadvantaged, it can change

their perspective. They're no longer just fighting for what they believe in; they're fighting for their right to exist. When people believe they're acting in self-defense, they're often willing to go to lengths they wouldn't normally go to. They get scared and angry. They lose their willingness to compromise or see other people's points of view, because they're afraid of being taken advantage of or losing what's important to them. They shift into a mindset of "I need to protect myself and my people," and they aren't typically very receptive to hearing about how bad someone *else* has it. Caring about other people feels like a luxury when you're worried about your own team's survival.

Talking to someone in this state of mind can be like approaching a cornered, scared, growling animal. It's ready to lash out without warning to protect itself, because it doesn't think it has much to lose.

So what happens if *both* sides believe they're the oppressed minority? What if both sides are concerned about their own survival and see the other side's actions as a threat? You can see why some conflicts get out of hand so quickly and are so difficult to resolve.

This can lead to the most dangerous kind of us-vs.-them thinking. If you think that someone is your enemy, that's bad enough; but if you think that someone poses an imminent threat to you or the people you care about—if you're afraid of what will happen and feel the need to protect someone or something—you're likely to respond with every weapon at your disposal.

All people need to know is that they're being heard.

Thankfully, the antidote to all this is simple. All people need to know is that they're being heard—not just as an individual but as part of their team. They need to know that we're listening to their team's concerns and that we're not their team's enemy. They need to know that there is a way for their team to thrive through this dialogue—a story where their team can continue to be the protagonist.

Listening to the Southern Baptists

Even though I grew up Southern Baptist, most of the attendees of that marriage conference saw me as part of a very different team: *gay activists*. In that space, I felt outnumbered and intimidated. I was in the minority, and I wanted very much for them to listen to me. But I'd spent years preaching to others about the need to listen to our cultural opponents, so that's what I was determined to do.

As one attendee in such a large room, I didn't have the power to end the large-scale tension between those two groups, but I did have the ability to make individual connections. I struck up conversations with other attendees—always a challenge for me as an introvert, no matter how long I do this work—and I listened to their perspectives on how things were going. I asked about their backgrounds and why they'd come to this conference, and I shared some of my own story, emphasizing the Southern Baptist heritage we had in common.

In these one-on-one conversations, I got to know the individual stories behind the people who had clapped for anti-gay sentiments from the stage. Some of them had had very little experience with gay people like me—or with gay Christians in particular—and I realized that they had a lot of misconceptions about what "people like me" really wanted. Some were pastors, worried that they'd be forced to perform same-sex weddings against their will or be legally prohibited from speaking in the pulpit about certain Bible passages. (I assured them that I, too, was a strong believer in the freedoms of speech and religion and would never support such measures.) Many were surprised that a gay guy like me was so willing to listen to and understand their perspective, and as their defenses dropped, it began to dawn on some of them just how hurtful some of the conference rhetoric must have been for me. Several of them went out of their way to apologize to me.

And as they realized that I wasn't there to attack them and that we weren't so different after all, they asked more about my story and opened up more about their own. I learned that a number of them actually weren't all that comfortable with their denomination's inflammatory approach to these issues and that they'd really prefer something more nuanced, but nuance had seemed so difficult in the midst of the polarizing conflict. They had a lot of questions for me about what it was like to grow up gay in the Southern Baptist Church, and I realized there were many simple things they didn't know about gay people.

These conversations weren't long—they were just opportunities to chat in between conference sessions, by no means an ideal or uninterrupted dialogue space—but they were still powerful. As we asked questions, told stories, and listened to one another, you could almost see the rigid team-loyalty tensions melt away. I've actually kept in touch with a few folks from that conference over the years, so I know those conversations made an impact on people. And sure, maybe we didn't change the world in those moments, but if those conversations convinced one pastor to talk about gay people differently in the pulpit or helped one Southern Baptist father be more understanding when his child came out to him, I consider that a success. And I know from my conversations with other pastors and parents in other contexts that a lot more than that has come from these sorts of conversations.

Breaking down the team-loyalty barrier can seem like a lot of work, but it's well worth it. And with a little effort, we really can change the world with nuance and understanding, one person at a time.

CHAPTER 9

Are *You* the Problem?

A bizarre sensation pervades a relationship of pretense. No
truth seems true. A simple morning's greeting and response
appear loaded with innuendo and fraught with implications.
    "How are you?" Does he/she really care?
    "Fine." I'm not really. I'm miserable, but I'll never tell you.
    Each nicety becomes more sterile and each withdrawal
more permanent.

                —Maya Angelou[27]

So far, we've been talking about the team-loyalty barrier with an implicit assumption—that *the other side* is causing all the "team" tension, and you're the one valiantly working to cut through it. Surely if there's any sense of "us vs. them" here, it's not *your* fault.

Or is it?

The team-loyalty barrier is most obvious when we see it in others. But what you may not realize is that you may be carrying certain team-based attitudes of your own into the dialogue. That can come through in ways that poison the dialogue and cause the other person to put up emotional walls. Sometimes those walls show up as blatant us-vs.-them thinking. Other times they're subtler; the person may simply tell you what they think you want to hear rather than opening up about what they're really thinking. Either way, it's quite possible that *your* team attitudes are part of the problem.

So before you pat yourself on the back for all your hard work reaching across the divide, let's take a look at some of the ways you might be making the team-loyalty barrier worse without knowing it.

What's Your Stage?

In 1986, a researcher named Milton Bennett proposed a model for how different people interact with other cultures. What Bennett called "cultures" might just as easily be called "teams" for our purposes. Every group has its own culture—Republican culture, Los Angeles culture, video-gamer culture, you name it. Your family has its own culture. If I hung out with your family for a week, there would be traditions, expectations, and inside jokes that I wouldn't know about until they came up. I might not know that I'm supposed to take off my shoes at the door or that you have certain rituals at mealtime. And if I asked you right now to tell me all about your family's culture, there are probably a lot of things that would never occur to you to mention because you grew up with them and are just so used to them. It's your culture.

We live in worlds of intersecting cultures. When you're talking to someone on another social team, what you're really doing is interacting with a member of a different culture. Their beliefs, values, and social expectations are different from yours, and that can create conflict. What interested Dr. Bennett was how people handle that difference and whether we're able to reach across those lines to successfully communicate and interact across the divide.

Dr. Bennett's proposal, the Developmental Model of Intercultural Sensitivity (DMIS), is widely used today in research on cross-cultural communication.[28] According to this model, there are six stages, or levels of growth, in people's ability to engage with other cultures. The first three stages—one, two, and three—all represent significant problems that can actually make the team-loyalty barrier worse, while the more advanced stages—four, five, and six—are where the most genuine and powerful cross-cultural engagement occurs.

For our purposes here, the details of those final three stages aren't important. What is important is that we move beyond the mistakes of stages one, two, and three, because as long as we're making those mistakes, we're making the team-loyalty barrier worse.

Unfortunately, when it comes to the issues that divide us, most of us live in one of those first three stages—and even if you don't, you may still be making some of these mistakes from time to time. See if you recognize yourself in any of these.

Stage One: Denial of Difference

My dad loves spaghetti, so when I was little, we had spaghetti often at our house. When we did, we always had it the same way. In one pot, my mom would cook the noodles, and in another pot, she'd mix up her special spaghetti sauce, combining a base of store-bought sauces with her own fresh tomatoes, ground beef, and spices to get it just right. When it was ready, we served ourselves, putting the noodles down first, then the sauce—enough to completely cover the noodles—and topping it all off with Parmesan cheese. We didn't twirl our spaghetti; we cut it. And when there were leftovers, the sauce and noodles went into the refrigerator in separate containers so we could repeat the process another night.

This was the only way I knew to have spaghetti. I thought that's how *everyone* had spaghetti.

Then, one fateful day, my childhood best friend invited me over to his house for dinner. They were having spaghetti. I was excited about this until I sat down for dinner and discovered they were doing it *wrong*. The sauce was mixed together with the noodles, and—horrors!—there wasn't nearly enough sauce. And there weren't any knives available to cut the noodles! Instead, I was told we were supposed to *twirl* them on our forks using our spoons somehow. What was this madness?

"That's not what you're supposed to do," I confidently informed my friend's oh-so-patient mother.

"Well, Justin, different families have different ways of doing things," she said just as confidently.

Really? Why hadn't anyone ever told me this?!

Most of us start our life journeys in some version of Milton Bennett's first stage, *Denial of Difference*. We're simply not aware that other cultures exist; we know only about our own cultural experience, and we assume it's universal. This is particularly true of children or people who have grown up isolated from other cultures. (On the other hand, if you grew up in a culturally mixed family, you probably have a head start here.)

If you're reading this book, you probably don't live in this stage. You already know there are people on the other side of the divide from you, and you already know that their culture is different; your question is how to reach them. But if you, like me, grew up in a cultural bubble, you may still find elements of this stage creeping into your life when you try to dialogue with someone from another culture. You might be shocked to discover that they see you as being on different "teams" when you didn't even know there *were* any teams.

Discovering other people's teams and worldviews for the first time can be unsettling, and your gut reaction may be to dismiss them as crazies and retreat back into your cultural bubble. But when you do that, you're planting your flag firmly in stage one and forfeiting your chance to get through to them.

The antidote to Denial of Difference is to maintain curiosity about other people's cultures and open yourself up to learning how other people see the world beyond your bubble. When you make a decision to ask that other person about their team and truly listen to what they tell you, you're stepping out of stage one and into stage two and beyond.

Stage Two: Defense Against Difference

Dr. Bennett called his second stage *Defense Against Difference*. This is the us-vs.-them trap we've been talking about so far. When I was shocked out of my stage-one ignorance by my friend's unholy spaghetti-eating practices, I landed smack in the middle of stage two.

Polarization makes a home in stage two: Our team is good; their team is bad. We're the heroes; they're the villains. When we paint the other side as undesirable and inferior, making unflattering generalizations about them while viewing our own groups as superior, we're in this stage.

The previous chapter focused on what to do when you recognize this mentality in someone else. But take a moment to consider whether *you've* been guilty of this us-vs.-them thinking yourself. Do you dread talking to people on the other side because you "know what they're like"? Do you find it easy to write them off as villains or idiots? Are you ever tempted to think that the world would be a better place if *their kind* would just disappear altogether?

It's very difficult to break through someone else's us-vs.-them thinking when you're stuck in this stage yourself. Even if you don't say any of these things out loud, people are perceptive, and they'll pick up on your attitude toward them and their teams. That translates into more stubborn, defensive behavior on their side.

Of course, this doesn't mean that you can never disagree with the beliefs, values, or practices of someone else's team if you want to get out of this stage. People at any stage can disagree with one another. But many of us fool ourselves into believing that's all we're doing, when the truth is that we're allowing our legitimate points of disagreement to bleed over into caricatures, stereotypes, and demonization of the other side. If you can't yet tell a convincing story with their team as the protagonist, there's a good chance this is the stage you're in.

It's an easy place to be, but it doesn't help us if we're trying to get through to someone else, because the more we look down on them, the less likely they are to listen to anything we have to say. Instead, we have to work to humanize them and find common ground—to begin to see them not as villains but as our friends and neighbors.

Stage Three: Minimization of Difference

How are you feeling so far? Do you feel pretty good about your ability to avoid the traps of stages one and two?

Well, hang on, because here's where it gets tricky. Stage three is where your best-laid dialogue plans will go awry. It happens to almost everyone, and it's probably happened to you, too. Stage three is called *Minimization of Difference*.

In stage one, we didn't know that differences between us and other groups existed. In stage two, we discovered those differences and wound up polarized. By stage three, we think we've found a solution: Just focus on all we have *in common* instead of what separates us.

It's in this third stage that people say things like, "We're all human; we're all basically the same deep down, with the same wants and needs. Let's look past our superficial differences and focus on our shared humanity."

What's so wrong with that?

On one level, there's some important truth here: We *are* all human, and there *are* certain elements of the human experience that are pretty much universal. We all know pain, hunger, and longing, for instance. In the face of something like racism, where some people are treated as inferior to others, this recognition of our shared humanity is incredibly important. When someone is stuck in an us-vs.-them mentality, giving them a chance to see and experience common ground with their opponents is one of the best things you can possibly do for them.

But—and there's a big "but" here—that's not the end of the story. If we stop at "We're all human, so we're all basically the same," we're missing something really important. Because the truth is, we're *not* all the same. We're different. And some of those differences matter.

In stage three, when we think about cultural difference, we

tend to focus on superficial things like differences in our food, music, or traditions. It's like a trip to Epcot or a world culture fair where you get to try different kinds of cuisine and say "hello" in different languages. These kinds of experiences can be great fun, but they're not a complete representation of the differences between our cultures. The version of Japanese culture I experience at Epcot's Japan pavilion is designed to be as comfortable and accessible to me as an American as possible. It's a very different experience from actually traveling to Japan and finding myself in the midst of a culture whose values, expectations, and outlook on life may differ dramatically from what I'm used to.

In real life, our cultural differences aren't just skin-deep; they're a big part of how we see and experience the world. And the most important differences to understand are the ones you can't experience at Epcot.

Our cultural differences aren't just skin-deep.

Take race, for example. I grew up in the suburbs as a white boy mostly surrounded by other white people. We didn't talk much about race in my house other than to say that racism was wrong and that all people should be treated equally, whatever their race. That was how I understood race: that it wasn't a big deal, and people who made a big deal out of it were racist.

I was a poster boy for stage three. I heard the racist, us-vs.-them attitudes of people in stage two—"My race is good; their race is bad"—and I saw how they fixated on race at the expense of people's humanity. I didn't want to be anything like that, so I went in the opposite direction and tried to *ignore* race. From my perspective, my friends of other races were just like me, except for their skin color. So I assumed that the best way to not be racist was to strive to *not see race*. If we could just have a colorblind society, I thought, that would solve our problems.

I actually felt pretty good about my approach until a conversation with an African American friend of mine rocked my world forever.

My friend Bolu and I were having lunch as usual when, somehow, the conversation shifted to race. Wanting to sound smart and enlightened, I made some comment about how we just needed a colorblind society. I fully expected Bolu to agree with me, and I was caught off guard when he didn't.

"I don't *want* a colorblind society," he said. "I don't want you to pretend you don't see my race. It is part of me. It's part of my life."

Boom. I had spent my whole life up until that point thinking that the best way I could fight racism as a white guy was to avoid noticing or mentioning race. It wasn't until that conversation that it had even occurred to me that that might not be the ideal.

It took me a while to fully process what Bolu said that day, and he was wonderfully patient as he answered my never-ending questions about his perspective. In the years since, I've had many more conversations about race with other friends. Each of them has her or his own perspective, but many of them have echoed some form of Bolu's words to me that day. Their race is an important part of their identity because it's shaped so much of their life experience—including, but not only, because of their experience of racism. So if I try to see them as people apart from their race, I'm ignoring a part of what makes them who they are.

This can be true for many kinds of groups, in many different ways. When group identity is very important to someone, attempting to ignore or gloss over it can cause them to feel like a big part of their identity is being erased. That doesn't help your attempt to dialogue with them. It only makes them feel misunderstood.

And this is how you might accidentally sabotage your own dialogue. Because in your rush to avoid an us-vs.-them mentality, you might wind up focusing only on what you have in common and ignoring differences that are actually very important to the other person. They may hold back, assuming you're not interested in what they really think. Or they may bring up the differences themselves—and then get frustrated when you keep trying to focus on commonalities. The dialogue falls apart, and you don't even realize that you were part of the problem.

If you're not used to thinking about all this, it can feel like a lot to keep in mind. But don't worry; there are some simple ways you can continue the dialogue without falling into the Minimization of Difference trap.

Recognize and appreciate what they like about their team.

When someone tells me that they just see me as a *person*, not as a *gay* person, I know they mean well, but it makes me feel a bit frustrated—as I'm sure my "colorblind society" comments must have made Bolu feel. It's true that I don't want to be seen as *only* a gay person, but being gay is part of my life experience, and it matters to me. Instead, I'd rather that person give me an opportunity to explain why that part of my identity is important to me (but without putting me on the spot and *forcing* me to defend or explain myself).

Likewise, if you have a negative view of Evangelicals and you find out I'm an Evangelical, take the opportunity to ask and learn from me what it is about that label that appeals to me. What is it about Evangelicalism that I value enough to make it part of my identity? Even if you don't agree with Evangelicalism, you may be able to find things about my *reasons* for being an Evangelical that you can appreciate and affirm. (You might even find that the word "Evangelical" means something different to me than it does to you.)

Clarify your language and learn theirs.

You would not believe how often I see dialogue break down over a simple misunderstanding about the meaning of a term. When we minimize differences, we often fail to recognize that the terms we use aren't always widely known—or may not mean the same things—outside our own bubbles.

Have you ever had an expert in a particular field try to explain something about their field to you—but it went over your head because they used a bunch of jargon you didn't understand? We all get used to hearing certain language in our own bubbles, and we can easily forget that others won't know what we mean.

I recently witnessed a huge fight between two people I know over the concept of "white privilege." They'd been arguing for quite some time before either of them thought to *define* what the term meant, at which point it quickly became clear that they had very different ideas of what they were talking about.

Be aware of terminology that's common in your bubble and take care to define what *you* mean by it. And when you notice the other person using terms you're not as familiar with or using terms in ways you wouldn't expect, don't be afraid to ask what they mean. (Believe it or not, even the term "gay" had a subtly different meaning in my church growing up than it had for my gay friends.[29])

Be aware of values and assumptions that might be culture-specific.

In strategic dialogue work, *values* are key. If you assume that someone else's cultural bubble has only superficial differences from your own cultural bubble, you may be overlooking some very important values differences.

The parenting techniques that one culture would see as ideal might be considered smothering in another culture— while *that* culture's ideal parents might be seen by the first culture as distant to the point of neglect. Some cultures value and emphasize independence more, while others emphasize *inter*dependence. What one

You may be overlooking some very important values differences.

culture sees as morally responsible sexual behavior would be seen in another as immoral and inappropriate. There's a nearly limitless list of ways our cultural values can differ.

And since so many of us take our own cultural values for granted, it's easy to walk blindly into a culture clash: You might be thrilled at the prospect of various nations coming together for a common purpose, while someone else might have been raised to believe that a "one-world government" is a sign of the Apocalypse. Thus, news you assume would make the other person happy might actually have the opposite effect. If you haven't paid attention to your differing cultural values, you're going to wind up quickly confused and frustrated when their reaction isn't what you expect.

Failing to recognize these cultural differences is one of the biggest ways we sabotage our dialogue efforts without realizing it. When you assume something is true of everyone but it's not true of the person you're talking to, you immediately make them feel misunderstood and defensive. Instead of showing them common ground and bringing the two of you together, you're doing the exact opposite: showing them just how far apart you really are. This causes them to cling more tightly to their team loyalty, and now you've just strengthened the very barrier you were trying to break through.

Of course, with so many cultural differences, there's no way you could dialogue with people from other groups without the possibility of some kind of culture clash at some point. It's unavoidable. What you can do, though, is to be aware of this possibility so that you can recognize it when it happens. Listen to how they talk and think about the world, and be willing to adapt what you say and how you say it to have the greatest possibility of being understood.

The information sources you trust might not be trusted by their team. The in-group terms you use might be viewed with suspicion by their team. The assumptions you make about how the world works might be totally contrary to their team's assumptions. When you stumble upon these differences, take the opportunity to ask about them and learn. Give the other person a chance, once more, to be heard and understood.

This even applies to things like personal space and conversation etiquette. My friend Chris grew up with a cultural expectation that people will ask each other questions in a conversation to invite the other to share their thoughts. I grew up with a cultural expectation that people will jump in when they have something to say. It took me a while to realize that Chris was often frustrated in our conversations when I didn't ask more questions to draw him out. I was expecting him to act like my culture instead of recognizing the differences in our cultures.

And this leads into one of the most important things you can do. . . .

Make a case from their values, not yours.

In an episode from the first season of *The Simpsons*, Homer Simpson buys his wife, Marge, a bowling ball for her birthday, despite the fact that she has never shown any interest in bowling.[30] Homer's the one who likes to bowl, not Marge, so he's essentially treated Marge as if she were just a clone of himself, buying her a gift that *he* would want rather than a gift *she* would want.

In the context of the episode, even Homer seems to realize that Marge won't want this gift; he's gone so far as to have his own name etched on the ball. But in real life, people often make this mistake without realizing what they're doing. They may think they're giving you a gift you'll love, because it's something they would love, but they've failed to recognize that you don't value the same things they do.

You probably know the so-called Golden Rule: Do unto others as you would have them do unto you, a paraphrase of Jesus's words in Matthew 7:12. It's a widely accepted moral principle, this idea of treating others the way we want to be treated, and many religions and systems of thought offer some version of this concept.

I love the Golden Rule. I strive to live by it. But it's possible to apply it too literally, missing the broader principle. If you asked Homer Simpson what he wanted others to "do unto him," he probably would have *loved* for them to give him bowling balls. By giving Marge a bowling ball (ignoring the fact that he put his own name on it), he might argue that he was following the Golden Rule, doing unto her exactly what he would want her to do unto him. But since Marge doesn't care about bowling the same way he does, his gift is obviously the wrong one.

Of course, that's not the intent of the Golden Rule. The idea is that you should treat other people with respect and compassion, taking their personal needs and desires into account, just as you'd want them to take your needs and desires into account in how they treat you. If I give you something that I want but it's not something *you* want, then I may be following the letter of the Golden Rule, but I'm clearly missing its spirit. And that's not helpful.

Some people have proposed a slight rewording of the Golden Rule, dubbing it the Platinum Rule: Do unto others as they would do unto themselves. Perhaps that captures the spirit a bit better. (Though I'd argue it's exactly what the original rule means.)

But whatever precious metal you assign to this rule, it's important to remember that what other people value isn't necessarily the same as what you value. Because as important as that is in your personal relationships, it's even more important when it comes to strategic dialogue.

That sounds obvious, but it's easy to overlook—and it's very often the reason an argument you see as incredibly convincing doesn't faze the other person even a little bit.

For example, I was recently talking to the members of a progressive church that prides itself on its social justice work. The church in question is one of the oldest in their community, and it has a history of being ahead of the curve when it comes to social change: The church worked to oppose racial segregation and support the civil rights movement at a time when these were still controversial propositions, and they were one of the first institutions in their area to actively support the LGBT community. For these church members, that kind of work represents a deeply held value of their church and their faith, and they couldn't understand why the evangelical churches in their community weren't moved by their calls to join them on the "right side of history" by supporting LGBT affirmation efforts.

For that progressive congregation, being "on the right side of history" is their bowling ball—it's what they value and the way they want to be known. They would see it as a great honor if people centuries from now looked back on them as having been at the forefront of social change.

But that is not a universal value. Many evangelical churches pride themselves on being *countercultural*—a moral "rock" in the midst of shifting cultural sands. From their perspective, cultural change might be good or bad, so pleasing future historians isn't a priority compared to pleasing God. It's a value system that can be very helpful in standing up to peer pressure but can also cause Evangelicals to lag behind other Christians in embracing cultural shifts.

When that progressive church calls on their evangelical neighbors to be "on the right side of history," they're making an argument rooted in their own values rather than one rooted in the evangelical churches' values. A call to be on the right side of history is a powerful and resonant argument for a group that values its social-justice work, but for a group that values being countercultural, it's just an invitation to dig in their heels and resist the change even more.

If the progressive church wanted to convince their evangeli-

ARE *YOU* THE PROBLEM?

cal neighbors to be more supportive of the LGBT community, they'd have more success if they based their arguments in principles those evangelical churches value most. For instance, they might argue that the Evangelicals' treatment of LGBT people has caused more people to turn away from Christianity and reject the message of Jesus. *That's* an argument that could get Evangelicals to sit up and take notice—and, indeed, it's an argument that has gotten the attention of a lot of Evangelicals I know.

The best arguments are ones based in your opponents' values, not necessarily your own. But to make those arguments, you have to be able to listen closely to your opponents and recognize what their values are. That's something you can't do well if you're treating everyone as basically the same.

> The best arguments are ones based in your opponents' values.

The Final Stages

Dr. Bennett believed that once you got past the Denial, Defense, and Minimization stages, you could move on to the final three stages: Acceptance, Adaptation, and Integration of Difference, each representing a greater and more nuanced ability to understand and interact with different cultures.

For our purposes here, it's not important to dig into the details of these final stages other than to say that all of us can work on improving our powers of empathy and observation; the more you can learn about others and see things through their eyes, the more effective you will be at combating team-based divisiveness.

But you don't have to do this perfectly in order to have effective dialogue; as long as you can avoid the traps of polarized thinking and minimizing difference, you're on a great path to overcome the hurdles of team loyalty and get people from the other side to take you seriously.

The Third Barrier

Comfort

CHAPTER 10

The Power of Your Story

The story—from Rumpelstiltskin *to* War and Peace*—is one of
the basic tools invented by the mind of man, for the purpose
of gaining understanding. There have been great societies
that did not use the wheel, but there have been no societies
that did not tell stories.*

—Ursula K. Le Guin[31]

If you're like me, you've got a mental list of things you know you
"really should" get around to one of these days.

I really should start a new exercise regimen.

I really should read that book someday.

I really should clean out that junk drawer.

My computer's virtual desktop is cluttered with icons of the
many files I know I *really should* get around to sorting through and
filing, and every time I look at it, I shake my head and think,
"What a mess." But it's still there. Once in a while, I'll throw all
those files into a folder, intending to go through it at some point
in the future, but it never happens. It's the digital equivalent of
sweeping everything under the rug, and once I've done that, it's
all "out of sight, out of mind."

Oh, well. Someday I'll clean it out. Maybe after I finish writing this book.

The truth is that we all lead busy lives, and we all have things we know we *should* spend time on, but we just never seem to get to them. Besides, it's way more comfortable to spend the evening on the couch. We can always get to that other thing tomorrow. Or the next day. But sometime. Definitely sometime.

If you paid attention in physics class, you may recall Newton's first law of motion, also called the *law of inertia*. In a vacuum, objects that are moving tend to keep moving in the same direction, and objects at rest tend to stay at rest—unless they are acted upon by a force. Human beings have a kind of inertia, too. We tend to keep doing what we've always done, moving in the same direction we've always moved, unless some force acts to get us to change direction. Echo chambers tend to insulate us from those outside forces.

When you ask someone to change their position on an important issue, it's the emotional equivalent of asking them to get up off the couch and go to the gym. They're comfortable with the views they have, views that seem to them to make sense of the world as it is, and you're asking them to do the hard mental work of reconsidering things, fighting inertia, and changing direction. But if they're happy with things as they are, and their echo chamber is reinforcing their existing views, why would they voluntarily take on all the challenge and uncertainty you're offering them? In many cases, they wouldn't. They're comfortable right now.

It sounds weird to talk about *comfort* as a bad thing. Usually, comfort is a good thing. We want people to be comfortable most of the time. But comfort with the status quo can be a formidable barrier to change. In many areas of our lives, as long as we're comfortable, human beings are inherently biased in favor of keeping things the way they are. Psychologists call this the "status quo bias."

There are a number of factors that could explain this bias, but a very simple one is this: Change can be scary. Yes, changes could be good, but they also could be bad. If we're comfortable with the way things are right now, why risk it? Why not stick with what we know? If it ain't broke, don't fix it.

Between our fear of what change might bring and our desire to avoid all the hard work of considering new ideas, sticking with our existing views seems way more appealing.

Still, our comfort with the way things are doesn't mean that we *never* change course. As comfortable as that couch is, you do get up and do things. People do change their minds, quit bad habits, and push themselves at the gym. And when we do these things that take us outside our comfort zones, there's usually a reason. You might decide to eat healthier and start an exercise regimen because of something your doctor said or because you were unhappy with what you saw in the mirror, but *something* motivated you.

Without that motivation, your best arguments to get people to change their minds are likely to go nowhere. The people are too darn comfortable. If you want things to change, you've got to shake things up a bit.

You need to give them a reason to be *uncomfortable* with the way things are now.

If you really want someone to consider a new way of looking at an issue, you need to give them a reason to be *uncomfortable* with the way things are now. You need to create tension for them that they can't resolve without reevaluating what they think they know. And the best way to do that is with strategic storytelling.

An Alien Encounter

As a child, I was deeply impacted by the 1982 film *E.T. the Extra-Terrestrial*. If you've never seen it, I recommend it—it's a classic.

In the film, E.T. is an alien explorer who is accidentally left behind on Earth when his team flees the planet. As E.T. hides from mistrustful humans who want to capture, study, or kill him, he meets a human boy, Elliott, and the two form a powerful emotional and psychic bond. Elliott and E.T. have a shared experience of feeling alone and misunderstood, and the film invites us to identify with both of them against the rest of the world and the forces of those who, in their ignorance, pose a serious threat to both of their lives.

E.T. is a compelling, emotionally resonant movie. It's nearly impossible to watch it without getting caught up in the emotional highs and lows of the story. We want E.T. to succeed, and we want those who oppose him to fail.

Imagine if, just after seeing *E.T.*, you learned that real-life alien explorers like the ones in *E.T.* were headed to Earth and would be arriving in a few days. How would you feel?

I don't know about you, but I'd be thrilled. I'd be eager to learn what the real-life versions of E.T. look like, where they come from, how they communicate, and what they can teach us about the universe beyond our own planet. I'd be thinking about the possibilities for sharing technology and knowledge. But most of all, I'd be ecstatic at the chance to meet a real-life E.T. and just get to know him. (Him? Her? Do they even have gender? Who knows!) Just imagine how cool that would be!

Suppose you, too, are excited about these incoming alien explorers, but when you share this news with your neighbor Dave, he responds, "Aliens? Coming here? We need to bring out the big guns and blow 'em out of the sky! Hit those suckers before they know what's coming!"

What's going on here? Is Dave a horrible person? Does he just enjoy the cruel treatment of other life-forms?

Maybe not. Maybe Dave has never seen *E.T.*, but he has seen movies like *Independence Day* and *War of the Worlds*—films in which alien invaders come to Earth to destroy humanity and steal our resources. In Dave's mind, that's what aliens do—they kill and destroy, and if we welcome them with open arms, they'll only see it as an opportunity to strike first. The only reasonable response, then, is to make sure they never get that chance.

You and Dave have very different ideas of what aliens are like, how they behave, and how we should respond to them. And those different ideas come down to the *stories* that you've experienced through these very different films.

When you and Dave hear about the approaching aliens, you each have a different script that plays out in your head, shaped by the different stories you've watched on the screen. You're each imagining what these aliens will be like long before you know anything about them, and you're each playing a story in your mind about how that first meeting will go. The stories you've heard about aliens in the past, even though they're fictional, have already shaped your beliefs, expectations, and behavior before the real aliens have an opportunity to show you anything about themselves.

So what do you do if you want to change Dave's mind about the approaching alien spaceship? What if Dave has influence over the government's response to this situation, and you're terrified that "bringing out the big guns" could start an interplanetary war—or, at the very least, destroy our opportunity to learn more about the universe?

You could try religious arguments, such as quoting Bible passages about loving others. You could try legal arguments, arguing that even aliens should be considered innocent until proven guilty. You could try scientific arguments about the important discoveries we stand to make by cooperating across the galaxy.

But how far do you think any of these arguments would go

with someone who is terrified that the planet is about to be destroyed by otherworldly invaders?

"Dave," you might say, "let's not be hasty. These aliens might be here on a mission of peace."

"That's what they want you to think," he snaps, his head full of images of burning buildings and unstoppable alien weapons. "We can't let our guard down."

"Everyone's got a right to be heard," you counter, switching tactics.

"I'm not gonna let them hurt my family!" he says, still focused on the horrifying images in his head.

The conversation continues in this vein. No matter what argument you bring up, however convincing it is to you, he keeps coming back to the same thing: These aliens are a threat to him and his loved ones. Therefore, they must die.

Dave is stubborn. But can you blame him? The only stories he knows depict aliens as bloodthirsty and merciless. He's afraid, and he wants to protect those closest to him. No moral, legal, ethical, religious, or philosophical argument you can possibly make is going to break through that.

So what on Earth can you do?

You can sit down with Dave and watch *E.T.*

Rather than arguing with him about the logic of the situation, give him a chance to experience a different story, to *identify* with an alien and have a new script in his head when he thinks about aliens. Seeing *E.T.* won't remove the scripts in his head from *Independence Day* and *War of the Worlds*, but it will give him a new, more nuanced perspective. And once he's had a chance to witness E.T.'s story, he just might be more open to seeing your arguments in a different light.

A lot of people are like Dave. They have strong feelings about issues because of the scripts in their heads. They may be afraid of what will happen if you or people like you get your way. They may even see certain groups of people as dangerous enemies, intent on destroying everything of value to them. So if some people seem stubborn and unreasonable, it may be in part because they have emotional or scary stories playing out in their minds. And you can't fight those stories with logic alone. You have to give them other stories—to show them another side of the issue.

Stories can change hearts and minds—for better or worse—in a way that logical arguments can't even touch. That's why strategic storytelling is all about using stories instead of solely logic to make your case. Rather than just offering *statistics* about poverty, tell *stories* about specific people who've been impacted by it. Rather than just arguing that certain behavior is morally wrong, tell stories of the damage you've seen done by allowing the behavior to go unchecked. Tell aspirational stories, too—stories of what can happen when things go right, to give us something to hope and work for.

Almost any logical argument can be made more effective with an emotionally resonant story. And unlike traditional arguments, it's tough to argue with a story. I can say that your logic or statistics are wrong, but your story is still your story. I might not agree with your stance on an issue, but I can't argue with the story of how you or someone you know was directly affected by it. The more you can base your case on stories, the more effective you'll be.

> The more you can base your case on stories, the more effective you'll be.

Finding Your Story

Stories are the most powerful way to combat the comfort barrier, and the most powerful story of all is your own.

At first, you might not think you have a story—or at least not one worth telling. Unlike E.T., there's probably not a Spielberg-directed film about your life. But you *do* have a story. And determining what that story is, and how most effectively to tell it, is key to changing people's attitudes—and possibly even the world.

At its heart, storytelling is your opportunity to give your cultural opponent a new lens through which to see the world. Up to this point, you've been focusing on trying to see the world through their eyes and telling stories about *them* that allow them to be the protagonist and help you see the world as they see it. Now, it's your turn to help them see the world through *your* eyes and understand why this issue or situation is so important to you.

Let's start with a little thought exercise: If I asked you the question "Why do you care so much about this issue?," what would you tell me?

Don't just tell me why the issue is important. Why do *you* care so much about it? What makes it so important to *you*?

Is it an issue that affects you personally in some way? Has this issue crossed your path in a way that it hasn't crossed others'? There's a story there.

Has the issue impacted someone you know? In what way? When did *you* learn about it? There's a story there.

When did you first realize how important this issue was? What happened to make you more aware of the issue or to change your mind about it? There's a story there.

Your story is ultimately the story of *the reason you care about this issue*.

Focus your story on one person—usually yourself.

Personal stories—those that focus on one person's experience—are much more effective than other kinds of stories because it's easier for an audience to connect with one person than to connect with a crowd. It's more powerful to focus on E.T.'s individual story than the story of his entire planet. This is why, for instance, charities that work to feed hungry children will often invite donors to "adopt" a single child and focus on that child's well-being rather than try to grapple with the enormity of the hunger crisis in a particular country. When Spielberg made *Schindler's List*, about the horrors of the Holocaust, he brilliantly drove home the emotional impact by allowing us to identify with a single little girl in a red coat out of the millions of suffering and dying people. We get overwhelmed when we try to think about large numbers of people at once; we're more moved by the story of one hurting person than we are by statistics about millions of hurting people.

This is especially true if the issue you want to talk about is an issue that has affected you personally. I care about finding cures for brain disease because I lost my mom to a brain disease and had to watch her suffer for years. I care about the future of Christianity in America because my faith has been so important in my life and also because I've seen firsthand how it can be twisted to hurt people. If you've been personally impacted by the issue, the story of its impact on you is more powerful than all the statistics and other people's stories you can dig up on the internet.

But even if the reason you care is something far removed from you personally, you still have a personal story about it. Maybe you care because of a documentary you saw on the subject that really impacted you. If so, your story might be about watching that documentary—and about both the powerful stories in the documentary and your *own* emotions while watching it and realizing how important the subject is.

Kick it off with commonalities.

Right from the start, your story is a great opportunity to get people out of us-vs.-them thinking by helping your audience identify with you instead of seeing you as an "other."

As you begin your story, emphasize the things you have in common with your audience and their team. Whatever shared experiences, values, or identity you may have, find ways to incorporate that in your story early on; this gives your audience more ways to identify with you so that when you get to parts of your story that are different from theirs, it's easier for them to imagine themselves in your shoes.

> Emphasize the things you have in common with your audience and their team.

When I talk to Evangelicals about my experience as a gay man, I always start by talking about my evangelical upbringing and how those values have shaped who I am today.

It can be tempting for me to start my story with who I am *today* and the ways that my life now is different from theirs. As a gay man, I'm often an outsider in evangelical spaces, so it would be easy for me to start with that feeling of being an outsider. But if I do that, I'm starting out in an us-vs.-them mentality, giving them every reason to see me as an antagonist before they even hear my story. That's the opposite of what I want.

Instead, I begin my story with a time before I even knew I was different from my evangelical friends. I talk about how important my faith was (and is) to me, and I talk about how my evangelical identity put me at odds with the rest of the world. These are things my evangelical audience can identify with; they are shared experiences and values for us. That way, when I talk to them about the moment I first realized I was different from other Evangelicals, it no longer seems like I'm an outsider talking about being different from them; instead, I'm telling them a story of something that any of them might have gone through themselves. And that makes all the difference in the world.

If you used to hold some of the attitudes the other person now holds, this can also be a great way to establish commonality if you do it well. Again, you don't ever want to come across as condescending ("I used to think like you, but now I'm much more enlightened"), but it can be helpful to talk about your past views in a way that helps the other person feel less alone. ("When I first met Barbara, I had never met a transgender person before! I didn't know the right things to say, and I have to admit, a lot of the things that went through my head were very un-PC. Thankfully, Barbara was very understanding and answered a lot of my dumb questions. My views have changed a lot because of her. For instance . . .")

Talk about your emotions.

Whatever the subject matter, the best stories have an emotional center to them. There's a reason commercials show people happily enjoying a product or having better lives because of it rather than just giving us lists of the product's benefits. A story—even an implicit one—with an emotional connection is more likely to have an impact on people. Years ago, Ellen DeGeneres joked about this in one of her comedy specials. "That old man who can eat corn on the cob again?" she quipped, referring to a denture-adhesive commercial. "I'm happy for him!"[32] It's hilarious that we would care about the denture troubles of a fictional character in a fifteen-second advertising spot, but we do, and that's by design. Emotional appeals are memorable and effective because our brains are wired to respond to the emotional arcs of a story, even if it's selling us hemorrhoid cream.

So if you have trouble deciding what your story might be, stop and reflect on what makes you emotional about this subject matter. When you are most emotional about this subject, what emotion(s) are you feeling? Afraid? Hurt? Excited? Worried? Protective? Sit with those emotions for a minute.

As you sit with those emotions, ask yourself about the *source* of those emotions. What has happened to make you feel that way? When have you felt that way the most? See if you can remember specific times in the past when you've felt these emotions about this subject matter. Pick one that stands out to you. What was happening? What was going on in your head while that was happening? Why? What was the context? How did you respond? How has that experience shaped your feelings today? That could be your story right there.

Don't forget that obstacles—and often pain—are an important part of any story. Sometimes, people are reluctant to talk about the pain they've experienced because they don't want to be seen as victims. But if you've experienced hardship because of this issue, the other side needs to hear that. If you've suffered, others are probably suffering as well, and that's important to highlight.

When you talk about that pain, though, remember to inject a little hope. Talk about how you overcame the struggles or how there's light at the end of the tunnel if we work together to change things. A story with no hope just sounds depressing, and it doesn't motivate people to do anything. Be real about the dark parts of your story; just remember to leave a light on somewhere.

Show the stakes.

It's one thing to give people a reason to care about an issue, but it's another to get them to care enough to spend time on it—learning where they were wrong, working to make a difference, and so on. The comfort barrier can make this particularly difficult.

So one of the most important things your story can do is to convince people that this issue *matters*—that there is something significant at stake. What are the *consequences* of getting this wrong?

In some cases, the other person might already agree that it matters, but they're seeing the stakes from the other side, thinking about the consequences if *you* were wrong. You need to get them to recognize the consequences (for you, for them, for society, for the planet, for someone else you both care about) if they don't change their mind and *their side* turns out to be wrong. What are those consequences, and why should they care?

A good story is about *showing*, not *telling*. As much as possible, you want to show those consequences through the way you tell your story. Rather than saying, "If your side turns out to be wrong, you're causing people to suffer needlessly," you want to tell the story of a person who is suffering right now, or tell about ways you've suffered.

This is easier to accomplish with some issues than with others, of course. Not every issue lends itself well to stories of personal, direct human impact that we can see. But try as much as you can, and try to keep it as close to home as possible—the consequences for you or for someone you know well, for instance, is a more powerful story than that of the consequences for someone you read about in a magazine article.

Show what's wrong with the status quo— without making the other person the antagonist.

Ultimately, the goal of your story is to give the other person a reason to reconsider what they've always assumed. To do that, your story needs to present some kind of conflict—something that shows why their previous approach is at odds with what you've experienced.

This is often more effective if you don't call it out directly. You don't have to say, "Your desire to kill extraterrestrials is wrong because I know one who's peaceful and good." Saying that just sets them up to argue with you. Instead, tell your story of meeting E.T. and watching him on the run from those trying to harm him—and then let the other person's brain fill in the blanks. You don't need them to admit to you in this moment that they were wrong; let them save face. Tell the story, and let them sit with that mental discomfort while they work through what that means for their existing views. There's plenty of time to re-visit this later if you need to.

But even though you may be talking about the negative con-sequences of their side's action or inaction, you don't want to turn your dialogue partner into the villain of your story. If you (or the protagonist of your story) suffered because of people on their side, try to distinguish your listener from the people who caused the suffering, implicitly suggesting that you know *your listener* would surely never behave the way *the people in your story* did.

If your story is about your listener, such as if you're trying to repair a damaged relationship with your dad and he's the one you're talking to, be careful to talk about his behavior in a way that shows that you understand his side of things: "I know you never intended to hurt me, but this is how I felt when that hap-pened." Making him into the villain only causes him to feel de-fensive. Instead, let him feel like a good guy, who, as a good guy, will of course want to help make things better.

How Long Should Your Story Be?

Your story can be as long or as short as you wish, depending on the context and what makes you comfortable. If you're going to be talking to someone off and on for months, you might want to share a detailed version of your story that allows them to get to know you more deeply. On the other hand, if you have only one shot at a single conversation with the person, you might want to plan on a short version of your story that focuses on a specific, emotionally resonant moment that stands out rather than spending the meeting on your whole life story.

What If You're Intimidated?

Not everyone is comfortable with telling stories. If the idea of telling your story makes you nervous, consider deciding what you want to say in advance and rehearsing it to yourself. I like to break down stories into a few memorable bullet points and then use those bullet points as a guide. ("I'll talk about my upbringing, then my struggle, then what happened when the church found out.")

In some cases, you can make an impact with your story by writing it down (or asking someone to help you write it) and sharing it online or sending it to the person in question if you're not comfortable speaking off the cuff.

But remember, ultimately, it's not important for your story to be perfect. If you stumble over your words or forget things you wanted to say, that's okay. You're not trying to impress someone with your perfection. Mistakes that show your humanity may actually work in your favor. The most important part of your story is the emotion of it. Just be honest about how you felt then and how you feel now, and let them see your genuine feelings. The emotion is what they'll remember, not the mistakes you made in the telling.

Storytelling, like strategic dialogue, is an art form. And like most art forms, there are no rules set in stone to tell you exactly how to do it. No matter what storytelling tips you might read in this book and elsewhere, keep in mind that the best stories come from your heart and have your own voice. If you're so focused on using a particular storytelling technique that your story stops feeling genuine, pause and take a step back. Your passion is what makes a story relevant to someone else, far more than your technical skill in telling it.

Like most art, storytelling is also something you get better at the more you do it. I know a lot of people who say that they're "no good at telling stories," as if there were a storytelling gene and they just weren't born with it. Nonsense! You know how to tell a story; you do it every time you tell someone about something you experienced. Besides, when you're telling stories strategically, you have an advantage that you don't have in most other storytelling situations: You can decide in advance what story you want to tell, and you can practice how you want to tell it until it becomes like second nature.

You might never become a professional storyteller, but you certainly *can* learn how to improve your stories to hold someone's attention and make an impact. It just takes a little bit of practice. Keep telling stories about why you care about the issues you care about, and see what people respond to. Over time, you'll find the stories that resonate most, and you can use those to help motivate people to care about the things you're most passionate about.

Unleash the Power

In my work, I've found storytelling to be the most powerful way by far to give people new insight on issues that matter.

Over the years, I've done a lot of things: social activism, media appearances, events, videos, podcasts, and writing. I've talked about Bible analysis, scientific research, psychology, philosophy, and theology.

But when people tell me that my work has changed their position, the thing they cite most often is my story—whether it's from hearing me tell it at a speaking engagement or from reading it in my book *Torn*.

Those other things are still important, of course. Sometimes it really does come down to a question of Bible interpretation or scientific evidence. But it's the *story* that first gets most people to care enough to want to learn about those things.

And the truth is, although many people have told me that my story was powerful enough to change their minds on such divisive issues, my story isn't all that unique. I know many people who could tell stories very similar to mine. Ultimately, *the most powerful story is the one that is told.* So tell your story—whatever it is—and unleash its power to change how others see the world.

The most powerful story is the one that is told.

The Fourth Barrier

Misinformation

CHAPTER 11

Fighting Falsehood

What is truth?

—Pontius Pilate[33]

In late 2001, following the 9/11 terrorist attacks, Dr Pepper released a patriotic can design intended to share a message of American unity. The can featured a stylized image of the Statue of Liberty with three words—"One Nation . . . Indivisible"—running around the top of the can.

The design sparked an unintended controversy when some people objected to the ellipsis, seeing it as an attempt to exclude the words "under God." An email complaining about the design began circulating, but the email's wording wasn't very clear—it gave the false impression that Dr Pepper had printed the *entire* Pledge of Allegiance on the can, removing only the words "under God." To make matters worse, somewhere along the way, someone—perhaps thinking Dr Pepper was a Pepsi product—altered the message to claim *Pepsi* had put out the can. (It was, in fact, produced by Dr Pepper/Seven Up, Inc., then a division of Cadbury Schweppes, not by Coke or Pepsi.) The controversy got big enough that Dr Pepper had to put a statement on their website about it. Eventually, so did Pepsi.

By February 2002, the can was retired from production, but email forwards about it were still going strong. The controversy continued on the internet for years, with emails continuing to claim this was something new, misrepresenting what the "something" was, and misidentifying the company involved. Long after the can was gone from shelves, I was continuing to hear about it from friends and acquaintances who had never even seen the can.

At the time, I was waiting tables at a chain restaurant that served Pepsi products. When a woman at one of my tables ordered a Coke to drink, I asked—as I always did—whether Pepsi was all right with her. Typically, people said, "That's fine," but some people had strong cola preferences and would order a different drink.

In this case, I wasn't prepared for the intensity of the woman's response. "No!" she said firmly. "That is *not* all right. Do you have Sprite?"

"We don't," I explained dutifully, "but we do have Slice, which is Pepsi's equivalent."

"No!" she said again, growing visibly irritated. "I don't want *anything* made by Pepsi. Don't you have anything that isn't made by Pepsi?"

"Um . . . sweet tea?" I offered. Sweet iced tea is a staple in the South, packed with as much sugar as any soft drink.

"I guess if that's all you've got," she said begrudgingly, "but I am *boycotting* Pepsi. You should tell your manager that there are a lot of other people who won't be eating here if you keep serving Pepsi products. You might not know, but they're putting out cans that take God out of the Pledge of Allegiance. As a Christian, that's offensive to me, so I'm choosing not to give them any more of my money."

I already knew the story behind the controversy. A couple of years earlier, I'd written an article aimed at my fellow Evangelicals, expressing my concern that Christians make themselves look gullible when they buy into unsubstantiated internet rumors. Here was an example to prove my point, and I found myself torn between correcting her and letting it go.

I decided to try stopping the spread of misinformation. In my kindest, gentlest tone of voice, I said, "Oh, yeah! You know, I heard about that. Turns out, it was a misunderstanding, and it actually wasn't Pepsi at all."

"No, it was Pepsi," she said confidently and curtly. "I read about it. You can tell your manager what I said."

So much for my fight against misinformation. I desperately wanted to argue with her, but that wasn't my job, and it was clear I wasn't going to convince her anyway. I just offered a "Yes, ma'am, let me go get your tea," and left feeling frustrated.

The Fourth Barrier

Misinformation can be spread deliberately, or it can be a result of simple misunderstanding. Either way, in our polarized world,

TALKING ACROSS THE DIVIDE

you're going to encounter a lot of people who have gotten the facts wrong but are *absolutely convinced* they're right. That misinformation affects everything else they believe on the issue at hand and can prevent them from accepting anything you have to say. Somehow—assuming we've taken the time to get the facts right ourselves—we need to correct their misconceptions.

If only it were so simple. Theoretically, misinformation should be easy to fight: When someone cites a false fact, just point them to the truth—the accurate statistics, say, or the original source for a quote.

Unfortunately, if you've ever tried that, you've probably discovered that it doesn't always work so well. People stubbornly hold on to their original beliefs even after you've given them ample evidence to the contrary. They might keep pointing to one unreliable source or exception to the rule while seeming to ignore a mountain of evidence on your side. They might question the reliability of your sources or the soundness of your argument in ways you've never seen them question their own sources and arguments. You give them what you consider to be plenty of proof that they're wrong, and they wave it away like it's nothing. Once again, you feel like you're hitting a brick wall.

This isn't just frustrating; it can be dangerous. If someone uses misinformation to make a decision about which soft drink to order, that's not a huge deal—except, perhaps, to the company in question. But if someone uses misinformation to make decisions that affect others' well-being, that is a huge deal.

Suppose your doctor wants to give a shot to your child—but

the latest research proves that this medicine isn't effective at doing what it's supposed to do and that it actually carries serious and permanent health risks. Would you agree to give your child the shot? Probably not, and you might well consider finding a new doctor!

But wait: What if the information you read about that research was entirely wrong? What if, in fact, this medicine is *very* effective and important to your child's health, and there are *no* significant risks associated with it at all? Well, then, in that case, of course you'd want your child to have the medicine; you'd be a negligent parent if you *didn't*!

So many of our cultural debates come down to a disagreement about what the actual facts are. Do vaccines cause autism, or are they a safe and critical way to stop life-threatening diseases? Is climate change a natural or even fabricated phenomenon, or is it a serious threat to our future existence on this planet? What is true? Do we know? And if we do know, why aren't we all in agreement?

On some issues, there is a legitimate debate about what's true: There might be different interpretations of the data, and we can't be sure yet. But on other issues, the facts are absolutely clear—or at least they should be, to any unbiased person—and yet many people remain convinced that there's a good case for a viewpoint that is just simply *not true*. Information overload can make it difficult to know the difference between a legitimate debate and a manufactured one, between the truth from a trustworthy source and a well-crafted lie from someone with an agenda. As a result, we end up convinced that things are certain when they aren't or convinced that things are debatable when they're actually well-established. People keep holding on to misinformation that should be easily dismissed. And if we can't even agree on what the basic facts are, that makes it nearly impossible for us to have any kind of productive conversation.

This all makes misinformation one of the most formidable challenges we face in modern society. It can destroy reputations, change public opinion, swing elections, and even cost people their lives. If we want the truth to prevail, fighting misinformation is vitally important.

So the next time you find yourself in a disagreement with someone and you start to suspect they've bought into some misinformation, here are some tips for breaking through.

Discover the misinformation.

Before you can fight misinformation, you have to identify it.

In some cases, it's obvious when someone has fallen for misinformation. As soon as my customer brought up the "Pepsi" can, I knew exactly which misinformation she had heard and believed.

Before you can fight misinformation, you have to identify it.

But it's not always so obvious. Sometimes we think we're starting from the same set of facts and talking about the same things when we actually aren't.

There's a hilarious scene in *Fiddler on the Roof* where protagonist Tevye meets with the local butcher, Lazar Wolf, to discuss a matter of importance to both of them. The only trouble? They don't realize they're talking about two different things. Tevye thinks Lazar Wolf wants to buy his new cow for butchering, but Lazar Wolf actually wants to marry Tevye's daughter Tzeitel. After a couple of drinks and plenty of awkward silence, the conversation comes around to the matter(s) at hand:

"Tevye."

"Yes?"

"Uh . . . I suppose you know why I wanted to see you," says Lazar Wolf.

"Oh, yes, I do, but, uh . . . there is no use talking about it," Tevye replies.

"Uh, Tevye, I . . . understand how you feel, but, uh, after all, you have a few more without her."

Tevye balks. "Ah, I see. Today, you want one; tomorrow you may want two!"

"Two?!" Lazar Wolf responds with shock. "Wh-what would I do with two?"

"The same as you do with one!"

The website TV Tropes calls this gag "One Dialogue, Two Conversations." It happens in a number of films and TV shows, often to great comic effect. When it happens in real life, though, the results can be more frustrating than funny.

Growing up, I was taught that sexual orientation was a choice and that anyone who wanted to be straight could simply *choose* to be straight. I believed this for many years; it's one of the reasons that I believed for so long that I wasn't gay even though I was attracted to men, not women.

After I came out and made some gay friends, I began noticing something interesting. Many of my straight evangelical friends still believed, as I once had, that being gay was a matter of choice. When they heard that I was gay, they assumed I had made some kind of *decision* to turn my back on everything I had been taught growing up. My gay friends, however, thought it was obvious that being gay was *not* a choice. They simply couldn't imagine that anyone in modern times would think otherwise.

So when the two sides clashed on matters of religion or public policy, they were starting with two very different understandings of how the world worked. In essence, they were having two different conversations: one side thought they were talking about people making an intentional, rebellious *choice*, while the other side thought they were talking about who people *are* at their core.

When there were news stories about a rash of gay teen suicides, my gay friends understood this as evidence of how depressing it was for gay teens to have to deal with so many negative messages about their unchosen, inborn sexuality. Some of my straight evangelical friends, on the other hand, took the opposite message from the tragedy. Since they believed those gay teens could have chosen to be straight at any time, they were convinced that the *choice* to be gay had led to their depression and that, if anything, this meant there should be *more* societal disapproval of homosexuality so that fewer teens would make that choice.

This fundamental disagreement about the facts—is it a choice or not?—led to a complete inability for the sides to understand each other. My gay friends couldn't understand why the news of these suicides didn't seem to affect my evangelical friends in the way they expected it to. And yet as critical as this bit of information was, it only rarely came up directly in conversations between the sides. Both sides just assumed that the other side *knew* that it was, or wasn't, a choice.*

Misinformation is at its most powerful when it flies under the radar. You can't fight the false beliefs you don't know about.

In the conversation with Tevye and Lazar Wolf, each man is behaving in a way that seems reasonable to him based on the facts he believes to be true. And to each of these men, the other man's behavior seems odd.

This is very often true in our real-life conflicts. If the other person is behaving in a way that seems unreasonable to you, stop and consider whether they might be operating with a different set of facts.

Before you start digging into the details of your disagreement, take the time to clarify the basics: What is the situation you're facing? What courses of action are available? What potential consequences are there? Instead of just telling them what *you* think the answers to these questions are, ask them for their answers, and pay attention to any ways in which their answers are different from what you expected.

---

*The question of "choice" is actually a bit more complex than this, particularly when considering bisexuality, sexual fluidity, and different views within both LGBT and evangelical circles. I'm simplifying the argument for brevity.

At times, you'll feel foolish having to clarify these things. We don't think to ask, "We're both talking about you wanting to butcher my cow, right?" because it just seems so obvious, once the conversation has started, that we all know what the conversation is about and what the basic facts are. But often you may find that the other side doesn't agree with you on a fact that you thought was obvious, and if you don't recognize that early on, you may spend a lot of time arguing past each other, not understanding why you don't seem to be getting anywhere.

It's like the tag line from the 1985 cartoon series *G.I. Joe*: "Knowing is half the battle!" Just being *aware* of the other side's misconceptions can make a big difference in how you address your disagreements, even if you aren't able to correct those misconceptions right away.

Educate them without belittling them.

Once you uncover their misconceptions, it's important to correct those misconceptions in a way that isn't condescending.

This can be tougher than it sounds. When you spend a lot of time thinking about an issue, it's easy to forget that not everyone else has spent as much time on it as you have. Ideas that may be obvious to you may not be obvious to your cousin or neighbor or co-worker.

In one of Randall Munroe's popular *xkcd* webcomic strips, he writes about the experience of realizing a friend doesn't know something that "everyone knows." Every day, he estimates, around ten thousand people are learning a given, commonly known fact for the first time.

" 'Diet Coke and Mentos thing'?" asks one of the characters in the strip. "What's that?"

"Oh man!" replies the other. "Come on, we're going to the grocery store. You're one of today's lucky 10,000."[34]

Most of us don't respond with that kind of enthusiasm when we realize that someone we're talking to doesn't know something that we think should be obvious. Instead of treating them as "one of today's lucky 10,000," we treat them as an annoyance or make fun of them for living under a rock.

"Seriously? How do you not know this by now?" we say. But that doesn't make them want to listen.

To put it another way, think about the difference between second-grade students and second-grade teachers. Once those students graduate from second grade and move on to third, fourth, fifth, and beyond, the things they learned in second grade start to seem silly and babyish. "We've all moved on from that stuff," they think. "That was *so* last year." From their perspective, there's no more need for second grade; they're ready for more advanced topics.

But for the second-grade teacher, things look different. He or she watches that year's students graduate, but the next year, there's another crop of second graders who need to learn all those same things for the first time. Five, ten, fifty years from now, there will still be more second graders who still need to learn second-grade stuff, even though most of us have long since put all that behind us.

If you think like the second-grade students, you may easily find yourself becoming impatient when you encounter someone who hasn't yet mastered the basics of your issue. "Haven't we all dealt with this as a society?" you may think. And yes, *you* probably have, and the people you associate with may have as well. But there are still metaphorical second graders out there—today's lucky ten thousand—who need to learn about the basics for the first time. So put yourself in the shoes of the second-grade teacher and remember to take things step by step for new people even if you've been through this a thousand times before with a thousand other people before them. That's what a teacher does.

With that in mind, *how* do you teach people the basics of an issue without being condescending? One of the best ways involves stories.

Use stories to show the truth.

In the previous chapter, we saw how powerful stories can be for changing people's attitudes. Well, they're also one of the best ways to correct people's misconceptions.

When I meet people who believe that being gay is a choice, I could try to prove them wrong by citing research or statements from psychological experts, but it's far more powerful for me to simply share my personal story. As I talk about the anti-gay attitudes I held as a young man and the unsuccessful attempts I made to become straight, the truth simply becomes self-evident.

People can always dismiss an expert you cite or wave away a statistic, *but they can't argue with your story*. Whatever misconception the other person holds, see if you can find a part of your story—or, if need be, someone else's story—that disproves it.

Some kinds of misinformation are easier to fight with stories than others. If your neighbor Dave has believed lies about what aliens are like, it's easy to address that by telling E.T.'s story or the story of your interactions with him. But what if Dave has believed misinformation about something else, like poverty statistics? That's trickier, but there are still ways to address it with stories.

For example, you could tell the story of how you first encountered this statistic, the research you did to validate it, or how it surprised you and changed your perspective. This way, you're not lecturing Dave; you're inviting him on a journey with you as both of you are changed by this new information.

Or you could simply tell a story of someone whose life was impacted by poverty and then connect that to the statistic you want to share. Your anecdote doesn't prove your statistic, but it may address the underlying issue, like convincing Dave that this is a problem worth addressing without getting into an argument.

With stories, you can set the record straight without directly confronting the other person's mistaken beliefs and making them feel defensive. And that raises one more point. . . .

When possible, get ahead of the misinformation.

Normally, I always recommend listening and letting the other person share their side of things before you do. But there's one big exception: If you know that certain influential misinformation is out there, you may have a better chance of countering it if *you* bring it up before they do. This is one of the best reasons to research the other side's views before sitting down to dialogue.

For example, let's say you're a medical professional whose dad has just been diagnosed with a serious illness. You've studied all the latest research, and you know that Treatment A has by far the best chance of saving your dad's life. Meanwhile, he's been doing his own research on the internet, and he's stumbled upon a site promoting another option, Treatment B. You know from your research that Treatment B is practically worthless. No reputable doctor would recommend it. Unfortunately, the website is slick and makes it sound like a miracle cure. Your dad is taken in, and now he wants to forgo Treatment A in favor of Treatment B.

Before you discuss this with him, do your homework and find out what arguments that website is making for the effectiveness of Treatment B.

Suppose the website makes a big deal about an impressive-sounding study that "proves" the effectiveness of Treatment B. The truth, as you know, is that the study in question has already been disproven, and mountains of research go the other way. But if you don't acknowledge the rogue study, your dad will assume he has information you don't have. On the other hand, if you make too big a deal about disproving that one study, you might contribute to the idea that there's "evidence for both sides," when that's not really the case.

So get ahead of the situation. Before he brings up the study, mention it in passing without making a big deal about it. Like this:

"You know, there was initial hope for Treatment B, but there have been dozens of studies of it over the years, and all of them have shown that it doesn't work. The only exception was a study ten years ago that seemed to show promising results—until one of the authors of that study admitted he'd faked the results. It's disappointing, because it would have been great if it were true, but it turned out to be a hoax. Now, Treatment A on the other hand . . ."

By acknowledging this rogue study before your dad brings it up, you help him save face—he's not put in the embarrassing position of having you tell him he's citing a hoax study—and you show that you're already aware of the other side's arguments. This is much better than *ignoring* the rogue study, which empowers the other side to claim they have "secret information" that's being "covered up."

But What If That's Not Enough?

As you've probably already guessed, the tips in this chapter just scratch the surface. Even when you do all these things, you may find that the other person, like my restaurant customer, is particularly resistant to having their misinformation corrected. In the next chapter, we'll look at what to do when these situations arise.

CHAPTER 12

Why Won't They Accept the Truth?

The human understanding when it has once adopted an
opinion . . . draws all things else to support and agree with it.
And though there be a greater number and weight of
instances to be found on the other side, yet these it either
neglects and despises, or else by some distinction sets aside
and rejects; in order that by this great and pernicious
predetermination the authority of its former conclusion may
remain inviolate.

—Francis Bacon, 1620[35]

Maybe you tried talking to your dad about that fake miracle cure, but he just won't listen. You've given him every bit of evidence you can think of, but he keeps insisting that you're the one fooled by misinformation.

Surely no one wants to believe a lie. So why is it sometimes so hard to convince people of the truth?

Barriers to the Truth

When I tried to convince my customer that Pepsi didn't take God out of the Pledge of Allegiance, it was an easily checkable fact. I certainly could have proven that I knew more about the issue than she did, and even a little research could have shown that I was right. But she wasn't even willing to entertain the idea that she might be wrong.

Some of it may be attributable to ego protection. Perhaps my customer was embarrassed by the idea of looking foolish after making such a big deal about boycotting Pepsi. She may not have been emotionally prepared to consider *in that moment* that she was wrong—but maybe my comment prompted her to look it up and learn the truth once she was back at home. (Have you ever insisted something was true, only to look it up later and discover you were wrong? Boy, is that embarrassing.)

Team loyalty can play a major role as well. When a controversial issue is split along party or "team" lines, we can get so emotionally invested in the viewpoint we associate with our team that we immediately dismiss any contrary information as the other team's propaganda. In this case, my customer may have seen this as a battle for her faith against a secular world. Perhaps if we'd had more time to talk and she'd learned that I'm a Christian as well, that might have made a difference.

And, of course, there's always the comfort barrier. It's a lot easier to keep believing what you already believe instead of exerting the mental energy to rethink things. I might have needed to give her some reason to consider the consequences of getting this wrong—though that might have been a tough case to make about a beverage choice.

But even as you work to clear away those other barriers, you may find that some misinformation is just really, really sticky. Oftentimes, the other side will keep insisting, like my customer did, that they know what's true and that *your* facts must be wrong. Let's look at some of the problems you might be facing—and how to deal with them.

Problem: The Lie Is Simple, but the Truth Is Complex.

We live in a world of sound bites and clickbait. People are more likely to notice, remember, and share things they can understand in a matter of seconds.

Most of us don't have the time and energy to read every article we come across or research every fact our friends post online, so we often share or comment on things without verifying that they're true. NPR once posted a fake news story titled "Why Doesn't America Read Anymore?" just to see how many people would comment on it even when the article asked readers not to in an effort to see who actually read the article. Plenty did.[36]

Unfortunately, that gives simple lies a big advantage over complicated truths.

Politicians know this. It's how they get away with saying simple but inaccurate things like, "My tax plan will save you money!" when the truth is that some people will save money, but only under certain circumstances and at the expense of other things. They know most people will remember the short version of the story over the long one.

Even trusted news sources often oversimplify complicated issues to make them fit a time slot or serve a predetermined narrative. When the University of Exeter announced the results of a study into the effects of hydrogen sulfide in helping to protect cells from damage, some news outlets ran with headlines like "Scientists Say Sniffing Farts Could Prevent Cancer."[37] (The research did not study cancer and certainly did not say anything about "sniffing farts.")

This is especially true on social media, which favors simple, easily digestible bites of information over the complex, nuanced details. "Pepsi takes God out of the Pledge of Allegiance!" is going to get way more shares than "Dr Pepper temporarily had a can that used three words from the Pledge of Allegiance, but it is no longer in production."

"Sniff farts to prevent cancer!" is way easier to remember and more fun to share on social media than "Research at the University of Exeter has shown that the new compound AP39 protects mitochondria, the cell components that regulate inflammation and drive energy production in blood vessel cells; this is a promising step toward future research that may help with the development of treatments for various diseases, though there have not yet been any human trials." (Borrrring.)

This creates a challenge for fighting misinformation. If you oversimplify the truth, you wind up contributing to the problem. But a long, boring explanation isn't likely to get shared and make an impact. So what can you do?

Solution: Create catchy summaries.

Spend some time thinking of ways to distill your facts into short, memorable sound bites or images. Then connect those sound bites or images to the longer, more detailed information for those who want it.

This isn't always easy, but when you can do it, it will pay off. Try to find a simple—but still accurate—way to express the heart of what you want to say, and make it as memorable as possible. That might be a catchy phrase or slogan, an eye-catching chart, or an evocative photo—whatever gets the point across as quickly as possible. In the case of the Dr Pepper controversy, a simple image of the actual can might have been the best option. Then you can follow that up with the rest of the story or link people to a source with more information.

Just try not to oversimplify things to the point of absurdity. (Sniffing farts, indeed.)

Problem: They Think They're Already Experts.

Here's another challenge you may face: You know that the other person doesn't have all the facts, but they don't want to listen because they're convinced they already know it all.

This is very common. Most of us *think* we know more about a lot of things than we actually do know. This is called the "illusion of explanatory depth."[38] In reality, most of us don't know that much, but we don't *know* that we don't know that much.

This concept was explored in 2002 by cognitive scientists Leon Rozenblit and Frank Keil.[39] They began by asking people this question: "On a scale of 1 to 7, how well do you understand how zippers work?" Most people felt that they understood zippers pretty well, so they gave themselves reasonably high marks. (How dumb do you have to be not to understand how a zipper works?)

But then the researchers asked a second question: "How does a zipper work? Describe in as much detail as you can all the steps involved in a zipper's operation."

What would you say in answer to this second question? How much detail could you provide? Most people found that once they were asked for the details of how a zipper works, they actually didn't know as much as they thought they did. So when they were asked to rate their knowledge of zippers a second time, they rated themselves lower than they had at first. Once they were asked for details, they became aware of their own ignorance.

In their book, *The Knowledge Illusion*, Steven Sloman and Philip Fernbach point out that this is true of many everyday objects, from toilets to sewing machines. We think we understand them, but if we were asked to explain their operation in detail, we'd realize we don't understand them as well as we think. This is also true of bigger issues. Many of us argue passionately, for example, about government policies on the economy or health care or foreign affairs, feeling like we've got a pretty good grasp of the issues at stake. But if we were asked to explain in detail exactly how a particular piece of legislation is designed to function, we might find to our own embarrassment that there are more holes in our knowledge of the subject than we'd realized.

Solution: Ask questions—but be careful.

Part of the key to correcting people's misconceptions is helping them to realize, on their own, that they don't know as much as they think they do. If you simply say to someone, "You don't know as much as you think you do!" they're likely to get defensive and insist that they *do* know what they're talking about. On the other hand, if you ask questions and give them the chance to explain their knowledge, they're much more likely to realize on their own that they might not be quite as knowledgeable as they thought they were.

When I was in college, I learned that an effective response to people who believed sexual orientation was a choice was to ask them to explain *why* people like me would choose to be gay. Being gay certainly wasn't cool or trendy in my social circles, and when

I came out, I found myself alone, depressed, and uncertain about my future. Why would I put myself through all that if it were a choice?

Most people didn't know how to answer that question. Many of them admitted that they'd never really thought about it before. It was one of the most effective tactics I found at that time to get people to reconsider their misconceptions about gay people.

But you've got to be careful here. Asking questions in the wrong way can cause a backlash and shut down the conversation. Yes, in the middle of an argument, I could ask people why they thought I would choose to be gay, and it did force them to stop and think, maybe even admit that their assumptions had been unfounded. But it usually didn't make them any more open to continuing the conversation. Often, embarrassed at having been shown up, they'd pull away soon after. I might have won the battle, but it felt as though I'd lost the war.

Sloman and Fernbach had similar experiences:

> We have seen that a good way to reduce people's extremism and increase their intellectual humility is to ask them for an explanation of how a policy works. Unfortunately, the procedure does have a cost. Exposing people's illusions can upset them. We have found that asking someone to explain a policy that the person doesn't really understand does not improve our relationship with that person. Frequently, they no longer want to discuss the issue (and indeed, often they no longer want to talk to us).[40]

The key here is to find ways to ask people questions and invite them to discover their ignorance on their own, but in a way that doesn't embarrass them or make them feel stupid.

For example, if you suspect that someone has some wrong ideas about what's motivating you in a particular situation, you *could* help them discover their ignorance by asking them to describe what they think your motivations are and why you've made the choices you have. But when they discover that they don't actually know all your motivations—or when you have to inform them that they're wrong—this puts them in a very uncomfortable position. Suddenly you're the one with all the answers, looking down on them because they couldn't adequately answer your question. That's the kind of thing that makes people feel defensive and shut down.

Instead, you might try a slightly different approach: Suggest that each of you explains the others' motives as you understand them—then, *you* admit your own ignorance of their motives, or at least give them the chance to correct you on the things you got wrong before you correct them. This puts you on more equal footing and allows them to receive correction or admit their own ignorance without feeling as though you've shown them up.

The important thing is to always remember to treat them as the protagonist of their story, never as the villain or the idiot. Use questions gently in a way that doesn't make them feel stupid for what they don't know ("Have you had a chance to read all the details of this legislation? Because I hadn't until the other day, and I was surprised.") rather than in a way designed to trap them ("If

WHY WON'T THEY ACCEPT THE TRUTH?

you know so much about this legislation, tell me exactly what's in the bill and how every part of it is supposed to work."). You want them to be able to see their own ignorance without making it obvious that *you* see their ignorance. You don't want to embarrass them; you just want to give them a hunger for the truth they don't yet know.

This is a choice between "winning" and winning: If you want to succeed in bringing the truth to light, you have to give up the urge to "win" the argument by proving you know more than they do. Resist the urge to antagonize them or bash their ego. Let them recognize the limits of their knowledge, then back off.

> # Resist the urge to antagonize them or bash their ego.

Problem: They See Only What They Want to See.

Do you ever feel as though the other person has a double standard when it comes to evidence for their side and evidence for yours? Like they'll accept even the weakest evidence for their side without question, but they subject *your* evidence to an impossible level of scrutiny, taking any excuse to dismiss your evidence as unreliable?

This might be frustrating, but it's not surprising. In fact, we *all* do it to one degree or another, and we're usually not aware of it. It's called the *confirmation bias*—we're all biased in favor of evidence that *confirms* what we already believe, even when we're trying to be fair.

A famous 1979 study at Stanford showed just what a problem this can be when discussing controversial issues.[41]

At the time, the death penalty was a topic of major debate. The US Supreme Court had struck down capital punishment in 1972, and individual states had begun reinstating it with new laws to satisfy the Court's requirements. This was a hot topic, and people had strongly divided opinions.

The Stanford researchers wanted to know how people with strong opinions would respond to facts that might or might not support their view. They recruited subjects who either supported or opposed the death penalty and told them about the results of two (fictitious) studies that seemed to support two different conclusions about whether the death penalty was effective at deterring crime. One study seemed to support their existing view, but the other seemed to contradict it. How would opinionated people handle this information?

When subjects were given statistics that *confirmed* their existing views, they tended to accept the research at face value: Here was clear evidence that they were right! But when the subjects were given statistics that *contradicted* their existing views, they looked more closely for potential flaws or alternate explanations.

As a result, each side was convinced by the data that confirmed their own beliefs but managed to find a way to dismiss the other data without being affected by it. The end result of all this was that death-penalty supporters ended up *more* in favor of the death penalty after seeing both sets of data, and death-penalty opponents ended up *more* against the death penalty after seeing both sets of data.

The same set of numbers caused the two sides to become more polarized.

This is why, after a political debate, voters on both sides can be fully convinced that their candidate won and can then wind up feeling even more strongly that their candidate is the best one for the job. We all see what we want to see. If a set of facts supports our beliefs, we accept it easily, and we'll be quick to point to it as proof in the future. But if a set of facts doesn't support our beliefs, we look for possible criticisms or holes that might help explain it away. Once we've found them, we easily dismiss the new information and feel even more confident in our views because— in our minds—our existing views just successfully withstood an attack.

As the researchers put it: "The result of exposing contending factions in a social dispute to an identical body of relevant empirical evidence may be not a narrowing of disagreement but rather an increase in polarization."[42]

This is what makes it so hard to convince people with new facts. When there's evidence for both sides, people just become more convinced they're right. And in the age of the

When there's evidence for both sides, people just become more convinced they're right.

internet, there's almost *always* evidence for both sides. Anyone can easily search online to find "facts" (which may or may not actually be true) that support their existing view. It's just as easy for me to search for "climate change hoax" as it is for me to search for "climate change proof." So if I'm in a debate with you about an issue and I want to back myself up, I can search the internet in ways that will help me find information to support what I already want to believe—including criticisms of your side's case.

And with those factors in play, you're not fighting a fair fight; your opponent is nearly always going to give precedence to the facts that support their side while being much more critical of the facts that don't support their side.

Add to all that the social network "filter bubbles" that tend to constantly bathe us in posts that reinforce our existing beliefs, and we've set up a system where it's very easy to be led astray by misinformation but very difficult to convince someone to let go of it. It's self-reinforcing, and it's easier to keep convincing ourselves we're right than to take a hard look at the idea we might be wrong.

That's why, when you show your opponent evidence that seems to clearly support your position, they just wave it away like it doesn't matter. In your mind, the evidence for your position is clear-cut. In their mind, it's obviously flawed.

Solution: Use stories to make your point.

The confirmation bias is so automatic that people may think they're being unbiased even when they aren't. So arguing with the other person and calling them biased probably won't get you very far.

In fact, in some ways, being biased toward our existing views is actually very reasonable. If I claimed, out of the blue, that your best friend is actually a compulsive liar, or that eating apples is hazardous to your health, or that superpowered mutants really are living among us in secret, you would hopefully subject my "evidence" to some serious critical evaluation before accepting it as the truth. It makes some sense to be skeptical of claims that contradict what we believe to be true. You'd have a hard time convincing people to fight their own instincts here.

But this is, once again, where *stories* can really shine. Even with confirmation bias, it's tough to dismiss an emotional, well-told story. If there's any story at all that can help you illustrate your point, this is the time to bring it out.

Combining your death-penalty facts with a powerful story that illustrates them can make those facts feel more real to the other person. If you were arguing for the death penalty, for instance, you might offer a specific story of a crime that could have been averted if the death penalty had been in place. To argue against it, you might talk about a wrongful conviction or a criminal who seemed unfazed by the death penalty. By themselves, these stories don't tell us which statistics are right. But they can work emotionally to help get someone on the other side to

> Even with confirmation bias, it's tough to dismiss an emotional, well-told story.

take your facts more seriously instead of automatically giving in to confirmation bias.

Problem: They Keep Believing a Lie Even After Their Evidence Is Disproven.

There are lots of ways to address people's misconceptions. Unfortunately, even when people do hear the other side, the damage may already be done. Research shows that misinformation can continue to affect our perceptions *even after we learn that the information was false.*

In one famous study, researchers asked young women to complete a task, then gave them a "score" for how well they did, leading them to believe that they had either done very well or very poorly.[43]

After allowing this information to sink in for a few minutes, researchers then admitted the truth: The "score" each participant had been given was fake; it had been determined before she even arrived and had no meaning whatsoever. Subjects were even shown the schedule that had determined their fake score. After acknowledging that they fully understood that the results they'd been given weren't real, the women were asked to guess how well they had really done on the task and how well they might do on similar tasks in the future.

And wouldn't you know: Subjects who had been given a fake "good" score continued to believe they were good at the task, while those who had been given a fake "bad" score continued to believe they weren't as good at the task.

The made-up scores *continued to influence their perceptions*, even though they knew that the scores weren't real. Intellectually, they had stopped believing in those fake scores, but emotionally, those fake scores had affected their perceptions in a way that couldn't just be undone.

This concept has come to be known as *belief perseverance*. In many circumstances, once a belief takes hold, we'll continue to believe it even once our initial reason for believing it is proven invalid. In other words, even if I could have proven to my customer that the story about Pepsi was untrue, she might still end up with negative feelings about Pepsi. Deep down, she'd still be convinced that Pepsi was an anti-Christian company, even though her original evidence for that belief had been proven false.

Solution: Repeat the truth—again and again and again.

Misinformation, like roaches, can be maddeningly difficult to get rid of. Don't get discouraged; it's a process.

An oft-repeated marketing rule of thumb suggests that the public needs to be exposed to a message seven times—and in as many different ways as possible—for it to sink in. I'd take that with a grain of salt; I'm not aware of any research supporting the number seven specifically, and I'd wager that it actually depends a lot on the message and the context.

But the basic concept is true. In my years running a nonprofit organization, I learned that if I had big news to share, I could send out emails about it to our list, post about it on social media, dedicate sections of our website to it, and talk about it at our events, and I'd still run into people who, despite being on all the right lists and at the right events, still sounded surprised when I mentioned the news to them directly. Sometimes, people need to hear something over and over for it to register in their brains. This is why advertisers run the same ads with such frequency.

Repetition breeds familiarity.

It may be annoying to see the same fifteen-second spot over and over, but it sticks in your head when it's time to make a purchase. Repetition breeds familiarity.

Something similar is true when it comes to misinformation. When people hear something false over and over again, it sticks in their heads, and it seems more credible as they hear it from more sources. But the same thing works for the truth: Keep reminding people of the truth over and over again, in as many different ways as you can, and eventually, it will sink in. It might not take seven times—or it might take more—but the truth has one big advantage over misinformation: It's *true*.

CHAPTER 13

An Uplifting Story—Starring Them

Returning hate for hate multiplies hate, adding deeper darkness to a night already devoid of stars. Darkness cannot drive out darkness; only light can do that. Hate cannot drive out hate, only love can do that.

—Dr. Martin Luther King, Jr.[44]

You're in a fight with your friend Sheila. You found out that she's been giving her time and money to support an organization that is against everything you stand for. You're angry and hurt. How could this woman you've known for so long be *helping* the *enemy*? Didn't she know how much this would upset you? You just don't get it.

You try to talk to Sheila about this, but the two of you just wind up arguing with each other. This issue is personal for you, and you realize your own hurt is getting in the way of being a good listener. You have a hard time stopping yourself from interrupting her. Meanwhile, she keeps getting defensive. You recognize all the signs of the ego-protection barrier, but that listening strategy that sounded so good in theory is proving to be much harder to practice in real life, especially when you're feeling pretty defensive yourself.

What do you do?

First of all, take a deep breath. Time for a little self-care. Take a break from the conversation to give yourself time to be alone and process your emotions before taking the dialogue back to Sheila. Do something to help yourself relax and clear your mind: Meditate. Pray. Listen to music. Vent to your therapist. Cuddle your dog. You can't think clearly when you're upset, so give yourself time to calm down.

Now, in a calmer state of mind, remind yourself of this: Sheila's position is not about you—even though it may feel like it is. Remember the story of Dave and E.T.? We all have our own narratives in our heads that may not always match up with reality. Sheila's responding to a version of reality that's in her head—not the version of reality that's in your head. She's making decisions that seem rational to her based on images in her head that *you can't see.*

When Dave says that he wants to blow those aliens out of the sky, it's not that he truly has anything against E.T. He doesn't *know* E.T. He's responding to the menacing images of aliens in his head. Likewise, the images in Sheila's head of the organization and issue you disagree on—and of how it all might affect you— aren't the same images that are in your head. You can't allow yourself to take this personally. This isn't about you at all; it's about what's in her head. And until you really sit down to listen to her, you won't know what's going on in there.

So let's say you go back and try again. You apologize for getting angry, you explain that you really do want to understand where she's coming from, and you give her uninterrupted time to talk. You practice all your best strategic-listening techniques, and you even manage to get to the point where you can tell her story the way she would tell it herself, with her as the protagonist. She's impressed. "Yes!" she says. "Yes, that's a pretty good description of how I see things."

Now, the mood is calmer. She's more relaxed and not so defensive. You have a clearer idea now of what those images in her head are and what interests are motivating her behavior.

But she's still supporting a cause that's very hurtful to you, and you'd like for her to stop. By now, she's feeling understood and ready to listen to you, so you try to make your best case for why she should stop supporting that particular cause. You use your crackerjack storytelling skills to tell the story of why this matters so much to you, and she seems truly moved by your story.

But then something goes wrong. As you start to get around to asking her to stop supporting this organization, she starts getting defensive again. It feels like the ego-protection barrier all over again—but didn't you already deal with that?

For a while, you felt as though you were getting somewhere. But now, even though she *knows* how important this is to you, she's returning to stubborn, defensive behavior, and you feel as though you've accomplished nothing. This is such a big deal to you that it could really impact your future friendship with Sheila.

So what's going on here? Did you do something wrong? Why is she getting so defensive?

Return of the Ego-Protection Barrier

Strategic listening, by itself, can go a long way toward breaking through the ego-protection barrier. When you listen to Sheila and help her feel understood, you really are making a big difference. But there's another thing that can raise her ego-protection barrier. When you ask her to stop supporting that group she's supported for so long, what you're really doing is asking her to admit that she's been *wrong* about something—and for Sheila, like for most people, admitting that she's been wrong is still very difficult.

When you listened to Sheila's story, you heard about the version of herself that she wants to see—the version where she's a protagonist. But if you're telling her she's been wrong all along, that changes the story. Now she starts to feel like a villain.

As we've already seen, no one wants to be the villain of the story, so it's easier for them to rewrite the story in their own heads to insist that they're *not* the villain and they really were right all along.

Psychologists know this phenomenon as *cognitive dissonance.* Basically, our brains want to make sense of the world, so if we try to hold two competing ideas at the same time—say, "I'm a good person" and "I've devoted years of my life to something bad"— our brains will reinterpret one of those two ideas to make them fit again: "Good people don't devote years of their lives to bad things, so that thing I devoted years of my life to must be good."

This can make it very hard to convince someone to change their mind on something they've invested themselves in.

The bad news is that people's need to protect their egos can get in the way of facing or admitting uncomfortable truths. That makes Sheila more likely to get defensive when you try to convince her that something she's believed or supported is wrong.

But the good news is that there's a solution. You just have to offer a new story that doesn't make her look or feel foolish.

Craft a Narrative of Possibility and Hope

Ultimately, when you try to get someone to change their mind about something, what you're really doing is offering them a new story—a narrative about themselves that you're hoping they will accept. You're saying, "This is the kind of person you are, this is what you care about, and therefore this is what you should do—the next logical step in your story."

That's what the effective salespeople at my electronics store were doing. Although they didn't put it this way, what they were really saying was, "I see that you are a person who cares about gaming. People who care about gaming buy this graphics card, because it improves game performance. Since you are someone who cares about gaming, this is what you should buy."

It's a powerful sales technique, and advertisers use it on us all the time. Ads tell us that this is the soft drink for people who like to stand out or the fragrance for people who are sophisticated and sexy, and if that sounds like how we see ourselves—or how we want to see ourselves—we feel drawn to purchase the product.

The key to getting around people's ego-protection reflex is learning to present your information, questions, and ideas in the context of a narrative the other person can accept as their own, where the image you're offering is one that they identify with or want to identify with.

Nobody buys a product marketed to terrible people. If the unspoken narrative you're offering is "You're a villain, so you need to stop being a villain," of course they'll reject that narrative right away, because they don't see themselves as villainous.

An appealing narrative allows them to feel good about themselves.

Likewise, if the narrative you're offering is "You're foolish and don't realize the obvious truth, whereas I'm smart and have it all figured out," that's also not likely to be appealing to them.

An appealing narrative allows them to feel good about themselves while still changing their mind, such as, "You're a good person who, because you value truth, will certainly be interested in this information I've learned."

Talk about their past behavior as perfectly understandable.

In your narrative, it's important to give people a gracious way to admit their mistakes and still see themselves as good people.

Saving face is a powerful motivator. On surveys, for example, people often lie to researchers to portray themselves the way they want to be seen. When pollsters ask people if they voted in the last election or how often they go to church, respondents tend to give answers that they think make them sound good or support their image of themselves, even when that doesn't line up with the cold, unvarnished truth. It's a form of ego protection.

So what would you do if you were a pollster who really wanted people to be honest? Survey writers for the Pew Research Center found an ingenious solution. When Pew asks people whether they voted, it asks the question this way: "In [the such-and-such election], did things come up that kept you from voting, or did you happen to vote?"[45]

Notice how the question allows you to save face even if you didn't vote. It gives you a way to admit that you didn't vote without sounding like you were derelict in your duty as an American. You didn't "happen to vote" because "things came up" to keep you from voting. Research shows that people are more likely to admit the truth when the question is asked this way.

Similarly, it can help people be more honest with themselves when you talk about their past behavior as *perfectly understandable* given the circumstances: "Of *course* you supported that cause. So many of us did! But now that this new information is coming out, I think it's time for all of us to rethink our support."

Or: "There's no way you could have known about the damage that group is doing. Who has time to do all that research, especially with a busy schedule like yours? That's why I knew you'd want to hear about this."

The point is, you're not blaming them for the past, so they don't have to get defensive. Even if you do privately blame them for things in the past, playing the blame game doesn't get you anywhere. It's better to offer them a narrative that allows them to change their mind and still save face. Their past behavior is understandable, and now there's a reason to do something different—and they still get to be the protagonist.

If I realize I've just cut someone off in traffic, I feel horrible about it. If I were asked to tell the story of what happened, I'd tell it in a way that allowed me to still be a good person, explaining how I'm normally a great driver but was just momentarily distracted, for instance.

But when someone cuts me off in traffic, I don't usually stop to think about how *they* might tell the story. I just assume the worst of them: They're a selfish jerk or a terrible driver who shouldn't be allowed on the road. And maybe that's true! But it's certainly not how *they* see things.

People are much more likely to listen to us if we can present a narrative that depicts them as protagonists: They didn't "fail to vote." Something "came up to keep them from voting." They didn't "recklessly cut me off." They were "momentarily distracted and made an honest mistake." They aren't bad people on the wrong side of an important issue—they were actually trying to do something good, and that means that with some new information, they, as good people, could shift their position while staying true to their values.

If you used to believe something similar to what they believe now, this is a good time to mention that—but be careful how you say it. When I talk to fellow Evangelicals about their anti-gay attitudes, I often make a point of talking about the anti-gay attitudes I used to have and how my experience changed my mind. This makes clear that I'm not laying any blame on them; I'm in the same boat. Just remember, make sure you don't do it in a way that makes you sound superior or condescending: "Oh, I *used to* believe the stuff you still believe. But I've grown since then." That just sounds as though you're looking down on them, which is only likely to make them feel defensive.

Show them how this change is consistent with their interests.

Even once people know you're not painting them as a villain, and even if you've made a good case for a new perspective, people still may have a hard time letting go of a past belief or cause they've poured a lot of themselves into.

This is a common problem. For example, suppose you had a little money put aside, so you chose to invest it in a small company you'd heard good things about. You buy some shares of the company, but it turns out that the company isn't doing well, and your shares just keep decreasing in value every day. What do you do?

Well, if there's no sign that this company will be able to turn things around, the *logical* thing to do is to sell your shares before things get worse. Yes, you'll have lost money, but at least you won't lose *more*. In real life, though, many people keep hanging on, hoping that things will get better against all evidence to the contrary, unwilling to sell the shares back for less than they paid for them and admit that they made a bad decision.

This is called the *sunk cost fallacy*. It's one of the factors that keeps gamblers at the slot machine or poker table long after they should have quit. ("I've sunk so much money into this machine. I just have to keep going until I win it back, and then I'll stop.")

Once we've put a lot of ourselves into a cause, it can be hard to admit that we might be wrong.

The same thing is true with our time and energy. Once we've put a lot of ourselves into a cause, it can be hard to admit that we might be wrong, because that would require admitting that we made a bad choice and that our time and energy might have been wasted. Instead, we fight to convince ourselves that we have to stay the course, that this thing we've been doing and believing really is going to be worth it in the end.

Letting people know that their past decisions were reasonable under the circumstances can help, but there's something more you can do. You can show them how changing their course of action is actually *consistent* with the interests that were motivating their earlier behavior. For example, I often talk about how the faith that motivated me to be so anti-gay is the same faith that now motivates me to challenge anti-gay beliefs. My *interests* have stayed the same even though my *positions* have shifted.

If the person you're talking to has been motivated by patriotism or economic need or a desire to protect children, show them how a new course of action is actually the most patriotic, the most economically beneficial, or the most protective of children. This way, they're still working for the same underlying cause, even if they're shifting course. That's much easier to swallow than "all your past effort was wasted."

Show how your solution solves their problem.

If you want to make your argument even more powerful, take this a step further. The best narratives don't just show how your viewpoint is compatible with their self-image. The best narratives show how you're offering *a solution to a problem they face.*

Again, successful advertisers use this concept all the time, subtly structuring their ads like short stories starring us—or, at least, someone we can identify with.

You're probably already familiar with the classic story structure that most novels follow. The story starts with a protagonist who wants something, then through the course of the story, the protagonist experiences one or more setbacks or obstacles standing between them and the thing they want. We, the audience, follow them on their journey as they seek to overcome the obstacles, ultimately obtaining what they wanted and resolving the story, typically having grown in some way as a result of the journey.

Many ads follow that same pattern in one way or another. First, we're introduced to a relatable protagonist: Here's a loving mom juggling her busy schedule and her family's needs. What does she want? To make sure her family is well taken care of. But, alas! An obstacle: Her son got mud all over his nice white shirt!

Whatever will she do? Never fear, here comes our advertiser's product to the rescue. With just one wash using their new detergent, the shirt looks brand-new and our protagonist's problems are solved. Thank goodness! Now she's an even better mom.

These ads work as long as we can relate to the protagonist and her problems. We think, "I've been in a situation like that!" or "What would I do in a situation like that?" And, if the ad does its job, we come to view the product not as just another detergent brand but as a solution to our problems.

And again, this is what the effective salespeople at my electronics store were doing. As they listened to the customers explain their individual interests and life situations, the effective salespeople put themselves in each customer's shoes, imagining what goals and problems this person might have and what solutions the store could offer to help them accomplish their objectives. This put them on the same team as their customer; instead of "How do I make you part with what you want [your money] and give me what I want [this sale]?" they were asking, "What solution can I offer you that will help you get where you want to go—and help me get what I want at the same time?"

Paint a hopeful picture of the future.

This is strategic storytelling again—but instead of telling a story about the past, you're telling a story about the future.

Ultimately, as human beings, we're driven by hope and possibility. We like to imagine ourselves in a future that's better than the one we're in now. Advertisers take advantage of this by promising that their product or service will make our lives better in some meaningful way, and in many cases, they fail to deliver on that promise.

But if you're advocating for something that really does matter, then by all means, talk about what that future could look like and what it will mean for both of your lives going forward to live in that better world and know that you've helped to create it together.

In the midst of conflict, we spend a lot of time talking about what's wrong with the world. Take this opportunity to be positive and optimistic. What is the future that you think is worth working for? Tell that story, and help Sheila see her role in making it happen.

Offer opportunities for them to help tell the story.

Finally, while there are a lot of lessons to be learned from salespeople, this isn't about selling a product. This is about reaching across lines of difference to find agreement and move forward with a shared vision.

Most people don't like to be told what to do, so if Sheila feels like you're just trying to manipulate her or push her in a certain direction, she's not going to be particularly excited about joining you in your cause. After all, it's *your* cause, not hers.

Instead, once you've had a chance to show Sheila the change you're hoping to make and why, give her the opportunity to help you dream about what that future might look like—a future where you're working together toward something that serves both of your interests. She might have some great ideas about how to accomplish what you want to accomplish or ways to meet both your needs.

Ask for her suggestions—about possible solutions to the problem, possible ways to implement the solutions, or even just what she imagines that hopeful future could look like. The more involved she is in telling the story of the future, the more likely it is that she'll feel a sense of ownership in that future.

The Fifth Barrier

Worldview Protection

CHAPTER 14

Making the Ask

Urgent optimism is the desire to act immediately to tackle an obstacle, combined with the belief that we have a reasonable hope of success.

—Jane McGonigal[46]

If there's one thing I hate about nonprofit work, it's fund-raising. I just don't like asking people for money. To be honest, I don't like asking people for things in general, and I don't even like *talking* about money. So *asking* people for *money* is a special kind of torture for me, like a Christmas-gift sweater that is both ugly and uncomfortable.

If it were up to me, fund-raising would consist of telling people about the projects and organizations I care about, then awkwardly trailing off with, "So, you know . . . I just thought you might like to know about that . . . just in case, you know. . . . So what else is new?" My first nonprofit somehow survived—and grew!—in its early years with little more than the digital equivalent of a donation box in the corner that nobody ever talked about. Thankfully, people were passionate enough to give even though I was a terrible fund-raiser. That wasn't going to be enough in the long run, though, so eventually I had to learn a bit about fund-raising.

When you study fund-raising, you have to learn a lot of things: how to set up campaigns, choose your goals, follow up with donors, and so on. But the most important step of any fund-raising campaign is "making the ask"—the point where you come right out and specifically, directly request a financial gift from the person you're talking to. You can talk all day long about how great your cause is, but if you never get to the point of actually asking for a response, you're not going to be a good fund-raiser.

This book isn't about fund-raising. (Thank goodness! I wouldn't be the person to write that book.) But the principle is still the same. If you're hoping to change someone's attitude or behavior, you need to know exactly what it is you're asking them for. What kind of response do you want? And if you can't get everything you want, at least not right away, what kind of response would you be okay with as a first step?

Generally, you'll have already set a private goal for the dialogue as part of the Preparation phase. Your "ask" might be a step toward that private goal.

But it's important to set your ask carefully. Asking for the wrong thing can derail your entire dialogue. Because it's at this point you're most likely to run into the fifth and final barrier.

The Worldview-Protection Barrier

It's not just our teams and our egos that we instinctively protect; it's also our worldviews, the beliefs we hold at the core of how we understand life.

Think about all the beliefs you have about the world: Does God exist? Which political party has the better ideas? Should children be spanked? Have people been abducted by aliens? Which is better: milk chocolate or dark chocolate? What did the ending of *Inception* mean?

Of all your beliefs, some of them probably aren't that important to you. On those questions, you might change your mind without much thought, especially if someone made a good argument for a different view. But other beliefs are pretty central to how you understand the world, and it might be difficult, if not impossible, for someone to convince you to change your mind on those core beliefs. Maybe you don't have a strong opinion about the ending of *Inception*, but you have a very strong opinion about whether God exists. If so, I'd have a much easier time changing your mind about *Inception* than about God.

But here's where it gets more complicated: Our beliefs aren't all independent of one another—they're connected. Your belief about spanking might be rooted in your beliefs about discipline, religion,

> Our beliefs aren't all independent of one another— they're connected.

violence, and/or child psychology. It might be rooted in what your parents believed about spanking and whether you believe they were good parents—or it might be rooted in advice you got from someone you respect deeply and whether you believe that person knows what they're talking about.

Now what happens when one of those beliefs is called into question? It can cause a chain reaction. If your beliefs about spanking came from your devoted study of the work of a noted child psychologist, but then I convince you that he was wrong about spanking, suddenly, everything else you learned from him is called into question, too. Depending on how central his work is in your life, that might not be a big deal—or it might be a huge one.

This is just as true for you as it is of the people you're trying to reach. Some of their beliefs have more weight than others, and some are easier to change than others.

Imagine your aunt Gertrude's system of beliefs is a great tree. It was planted when she was born, and over time it has grown and grown into something enormous. As long as she's alive, that tree will keep growing and changing, and all the events of her life play a part in determining how it grows and changes.

If you could examine that tree, you'd see the evidence of scars from past traumas, periods of more or less water, ways in which the tree has grown toward the sun. The older the tree gets, the more its shape is defined and the less noticeable any given change might be as a percentage of the overall tree—but it's always growing, always changing, always reacting to the experiences of life.

At the roots of Aunt Gertrude's tree are the beliefs that are most fundamental to her worldview. These are the beliefs that help define how she understands herself and the world around her. They are the beliefs that anchor everything else. It would be nearly impossible to change these root beliefs without dramatically altering Aunt Gertrude's whole tree.

The trunk of Aunt Gertrude's tree contains more beliefs. These beliefs are connected to the beliefs in the roots and generally grow out of them. The beliefs in the trunk are also very important to her, but they're not quite as fundamental. If something were to happen to one of these beliefs, it might still have a significant impact on Aunt Gertrude, but it probably wouldn't change her understanding of *who she is*. Instead, it might cause her to reevaluate other beliefs she holds and assumptions she's made through the years. These trunk beliefs are still connected to a lot of other beliefs, though, so making a change here is no small matter.

Growing out of the trunk are lots and lots of branches—large ones leading to smaller and smaller ones as they fork off in various directions. This is where most of Aunt Gertrude's less-important beliefs are. The smaller twigs might not even be firm beliefs; they might be merely assumptions about the world, based on fleeting observations or experiences. These are the easiest to change; a single new experience or thought-provoking conversation could easily shift one of these twigs without altering the larger, more established branches it's growing out of.

And finally, out of those branches and twigs grow the leaves that, in our analogy, represent Aunt Gertrude's public face to the world. These are her words and actions, the big and small decisions she makes each day. These leaves are our primary experience of her, but they don't exist in a vacuum; they're attached to assumptions that grow out of beliefs about the world that are in turn connected to bigger and more important beliefs, all the way to the roots of her tree.

I find this analogy helpful because not all beliefs have equal weight in a person's life. Some beliefs are relatively unimportant and easy to change. Others are deeply connected to many parts of ourselves, and we fight hard to keep those beliefs from changing. If they were to change, it would force us to reevaluate so many other things—including, perhaps, our understanding of ourselves and the world around us. That's destabilizing and scary.

Think for a moment about your own core beliefs—your own "roots." What is most central to your worldview? It might include your beliefs about God, religion, or the meaning of life. Maybe you have strong beliefs about what it means for something to be morally right or wrong. (Is it based on whether it harms others? Whether it helps humanity as a whole? Is it defined by a higher power?) Your "root" beliefs might also include beliefs about who is trustworthy in your life—the people, institutions, and sources of information that you trust above all else. There might be other kinds of things in your roots as well; in general, these are the beliefs you hold about who you are, how the universe works, and what matters in life. They are the beliefs that, if something were to happen to change one of them, it would affect you in a major way, and it might even change how you define yourself.

Aunt Gertrude's roots aren't the same as yours, but they're just as important to her as yours are to you. They are the foundation of everything she knows and believes about the world.

Now imagine that Aunt Gertrude's tree is in the yard right next to yours, and it has a branch that's sticking over the fence and dropping leaves in your yard. Those leaves are driving you crazy, and you'd like to do something about them. Which is the more reasonable course of action: to ask her to trim the branch in question, or to go out and start trying to dig up the entire tree by the roots with your bare hands?

Obviously, the best and easiest solution—for you and for Aunt Gertrude—is to focus on addressing the smallest possible branch that can get the job done. Yes, if you pull up the whole tree by its roots, that would also solve the problem; but with a well-established tree, you're not likely to be very successful—and even if you were, imagine the devastation for Aunt Gertrude when her entire belief tree is uprooted!

This may sound like common sense, and in many ways, it is. But I often see people unsuccessfully trying to change others' views by uprooting their metaphorical trees.

For instance, a friend of mine was telling me about her attempt to change her brother's mind on same-sex marriage. My friend supported it; her brother opposed it. During their discussion, her brother cited Bible passages as justification for his view. My friend responded by arguing that the Bible was thousands of years old, had been translated from other languages, and couldn't be taken literally.

"That's the moment you lost the argument," I told her.

I could understand *why* my friend made the argument she made. She doesn't share her brother's view of the Bible, and she believes his literal reading of the Bible—what my evangelical friends would call a "high view of Scripture"—is the reason for his disagreement with her on same-sex marriage. In some ways, she's right; his view of the Bible *is* connected to his view of marriage in very consequential ways. However, what her approach did was the opposite of what she wanted. She turned a disagreement about marriage into a direct disagreement on the Bible itself, something at the root of her brother's worldview. She might just as well have tried to deal with a problematic tree branch by attempting to dig up the entire tree with her bare hands.

Whether you agree with my friend's brother's view of the Bible or not, there's no denying our roots go deep. If you ask me to change my deeply rooted, long-held understanding of my faith, just think of everything else you're calling into question in my life. If I've dedicated years of my life to a cause, what does it do to my sense of self if you try to tell me that the cause was wrong? If people important to me died fighting in a war, what happens to my sense of their honor if you try to convince me that the war they fought in was meaningless or immoral or even that they were on the wrong side? These are the kinds of beliefs we hold in our roots, and while it's not impossible for them to change, most people will fight tooth and nail to protect these roots, because they are connected to so many other parts of themselves. The roots form the basis of their entire worldview. And that's what I mean by "worldview protection."

So what does this mean for you? Well, when you're trying to change someone's mind on an issue, it's not just *that issue* you have to keep in mind. You have to think about the relationship of that issue to their larger worldview, and even if you disagree with that worldview, it may be wise to pick your battles.

You can't just ask people to uproot their tree, change their entire worldview, and decide that they now believe everything you believe. Sure, that's probably what you'd *like* for them to do. I know I wish I had the power to wave a magic wand and make everyone else see things my way and stop believing things I think are silly. But I don't have that power, and neither do you; if you make that your goal, you're not only going to be sorely disappointed, you're also likely to send your dialogue partners heading as fast as they can in the opposite direction. To keep them engaged, you need to pick the right ask.

> You can't just ask people to uproot their tree.

Choosing Your Ask

Before you leave a formal dialogue setting, it's a good idea to set some kind of concrete ask—something specific and reasonable to ask for from the other person.

A good ask should meet two important criteria: It needs to keep things moving forward, and it needs to be something reasonable that the other person can do *within the bounds of their existing worldview.*

You don't have to get it all done at once; consider a "first step."

Your long-term ask might actually be multiple asks over a period of time. In the fund-raising world, people are often initially asked to make a relatively small donation, and then later, once they've established their willingness to support the cause, they might be approached about the possibility of increasing their level of support. In a similar way, your initial ask in a dialogue like this might simply be for the other person's commitment to continue the dialogue. Real change doesn't happen overnight; keeping the dialogue going is important if you want to see long-term attitude change.

Eventually, of course, you're going to want something more than just eternal dialogue, so it's important to know going in what you'd really like to ask for, even if you don't ask for it right away.

But whether you're considering a short-term or long-term ask, this is the question you have to pose to yourself: What is it this person can do *within the bounds of their existing worldview* that you would see as a step forward?

If you're talking to someone in a position of authority, maybe you'd like for them to endorse a policy change or set up a meeting with you and other leaders. If it's an interpersonal dispute with a family member, maybe you just want them to agree to hear your side of the story.

Whatever the situation, it's important to have reasonable, realistic goals that can fit within the other person's worldview. You might think that the other person's entire religion or ideology is nuts, but if you're not willing to settle for anything less than their whole tree getting uprooted, then you're almost certainly going to have to settle for nothing at all.

Consider their interests.

Of course, this isn't just all about you. There's someone else in this dialogue, and they probably have things they want, too.

Remember the example of the two people arguing over whether the library window should be open or closed? This is the right time to "focus on interests, not positions."

What does the person on the other side want? That's their *position*. But more important, *why* do they want it? That's their *interest*. Likewise, what do you want from them? That's your position. Now ask yourself, *why* do you want it? That's your interest.

The sweet spot for your ask is something that helps advance their interest as well as yours. If you're asking for something that conflicts with their stated *position*, that's okay, as long as you can show how it aligns with their *interests*. ("I know you said you want that window open, but I think I have another solution that will still get you the fresh air you want and solve my problem at the same time.") But if your ask conflicts with their underlying *inter-*

ests, they're probably not going to respond to it very well, and you might want to consider a different ask, at least as a first step.

Look at their interest and your interest together. Are there any points you might be able to agree to—things that help both of you advance your interests, even if it's not quite in line with your stated positions? Propose that, and see what happens. You might be surprised at where it will take you.

Don't assume their objections. Listen.

Even when you try to ask for something that you think the other side will see as reasonable, they might still object to your ask. If they do, don't get defensive or immediately start arguing for why they should change their mind. Instead, go back to your listening strategy and pay attention to the *reason* for their objection to your ask.

Pay attention to the *reason* for their objection to your ask.

In their book, *The Enigma of Reason*, Hugo Mercier and Dan Sperber imagine different versions of a conversation between two women about going to dinner. One version goes like this:

> Hélène: We should go to Isami; it's a good restaurant.
> Marjorie: I don't know. I had Japanese last week already.
> Hélène: But this one is very original.

Another goes like this:

Hélène: We should go to Isami; it's a good restaurant.

Marjorie: I don't know. I don't have much money at the moment, and Japanese restaurants can be quite pricy.

Hélène: But this one is quite cheap.[47]

In both versions, Hélène wants to go to the restaurant and Marjorie is reluctant. But Marjorie's reasons for hesitating are different in the two conversations, and that means Hélène's response must be different as well. If Hélène wants to convince Marjorie to go to the restaurant, she needs to tailor her argument to address Marjorie's needs and wants.

To effectively convince someone of something, we need to listen to their wants and needs and build our response on that feedback. If we're just deciding where to go to eat, this is such a simple and obvious thing that we don't even think about it. But with weightier, more emotional issues, it's easy for this process to break down. People on both sides get so focused on the rightness or wrongness of a particular argument that they fail to adequately explain or listen to the underlying concerns behind their positions.

Imagine if Marjorie had responded to Hélène's suggestion only by saying, "No, I'd rather not go there," without clarifying her reasons—and Hélène had simply charged ahead with one argument after another about the uniqueness of the décor or the freshness of the fish, not realizing that Marjorie's real concern was about money. Hélène's arguments would be totally ineffective, and both women might well wind up getting irritated with each other.

That seems obvious, doesn't it? But when we're arguing about the issues we care about most, it's easy to forget. We make the same arguments to everyone, usually based on our own wants, needs, and values, and we completely fail to take their individual motivations or concerns into account. Our arguments go nowhere, and both sides get frustrated, both feeling as though they're not being heard.

If you're trying to convince a local business owner to change a harmful company policy, for instance, it's important to understand why that business owner might be resistant. Is she concerned that the change would cost too much? That it would generate negative publicity among her core customers? That it would violate her own personal values? Showing her that the policy change would bring in new customers might be a strong argument if her concern is about money, but it's not going to help much if her concern is about values. On the other hand, the values conversation may be significantly less helpful if she's worried about losing business. (As Veronica, the snarky boss of TV's *Better Off Ted* put it, "How will we ever make the Fortune 500 list of the most moral companies? Oh wait. They don't have that.")[48]

If the other person doesn't give any reason for their objection, see if you can find a way to learn what they're thinking without putting them on the spot. (It's probably not going to help matters if you just blurt out, "Why not?") For instance, you might ask them for an alternative proposal they'd be more comfortable with and see what it is they like better about that proposal. Once you know what's motivating their objection, you're in a better position to modify your ask to address their objections—or at least make a more effective case for it.

Be open to reasonable compromise.

The goal of strategic dialogue is to allow both sides to hear each other well enough to get past all those barriers and let the truth shine—and ideally, that means both sides can come together and agree on a path forward.

But we all know we don't live in an ideal world. People's minds take time to change, so you may find that the other person just isn't in a good position to give you any of the things you want to ask for. What do you ask for if you're still so far apart that nothing you want is realistic?

Even with strategic dialogue, compromise is sometimes necessary. Insisting on getting everything 100 percent your way—even if you are completely in the right and *deserve* to get everything your way—can shut down the dialogue and cause you to get zero percent your way. The perfect is the enemy of the good.

Even with strategic dialogue, compromise is sometimes necessary.

Easy to say. But it's not always so simple, is it?

I remember when, as a kid, I first heard about wars over land in the Middle East. I didn't understand why they couldn't just be worked out. Surely, I thought, both sides could see that they had more to gain by sitting down together and negotiating some kind of compromise. Surely ongoing fighting was not in anyone's interest. But these wars have complex roots. The fighting continues.

To children, these things seem simple. As an adult, though, I've seen many situations where neither side in an argument wanted to compromise because neither side thought they had done anything wrong. Both saw themselves as the wronged party, and both thought that any form of compromise was to accept less than their due—less than justice. I've seen families and friendships permanently destroyed because neither side was willing to give in, each convinced that the rift was entirely the fault of the other.

We see it easily when it affects others, but we fall victim to it just the same when we're on one of the sides. "This is different," we tell ourselves, "because in this situation, I'm totally in the right." And, again, maybe we are! Just because both sides *think* they're in the right doesn't mean they're both *actually* equally to blame for the fight. One side might be completely wrong. The end result is still the same, because the people on the other side think they're right.

But here's where I believe strategic dialogue is so different from the form of compromise most of us were taught growing up. With traditional compromise, you agree to "meet in the middle," and you settle for something less than you deserve—maybe even less than you need. Negotiation tactics are often about pushing that meeting point more in your direction so you can get more of what you want—and, when possible, finding shared interests and creative solutions. Even with all the best negotiation tactics, though, you may still be left with a compromise that gives you less than you need or want or deserve on an issue that is too important to be left to a "meet in the middle"–style compromise.

Traditional compromise leaves you there, settling for what you can get. Strategic dialogue goes a step further, though. It says, "Okay, take that compromise, however large or small, as an important step in the right direction. But also *commit to stay in the dialogue*. Because as long as you both stay in the dialogue, you can keep working for greater understanding and better solutions."

I always try to think in terms of giving people "on-ramps" to the discussion—a way to get from where they currently are to where I'd like them to be. Those on-ramps can take a number of forms. Typically, it means having the conversation with them in a way that challenges their misconceptions and encourages them to grow in their understanding, without pushing them so far outside of their comfort zone that they stop engaging.

It can be too much to ask someone to learn new language, accept new facts, and change their long-held beliefs all at the same time. That's okay; you don't have to do it all at once. Sometimes just getting them to have a conversation with you that doesn't involve screaming (or that involves less screaming than usual) may be a major accomplishment.

If you can't get anything significant at the end of the conversation, ask for a baby step: some small step forward, even though it's far less than you want. If you can't even get a baby step, ask for a commitment to continue the dialogue in the future. As long as both sides are committed to continue the dialogue, you can continue the work of attitude change. And as you both take time to think over how things went in the dialogue, all sorts of epiphanies can occur.

CHAPTER 15

Reflection

*I wanted you to see what real courage is, instead of getting
the idea that courage is a man with a gun in his hand. It's
when you know you're licked before you begin, but you begin
anyway and see it through no matter what.*

—Atticus Finch, in Harper Lee's *To Kill a Mockingbird*[49]

BASIC STEPS OF STRATEGIC DIALOGUE

A. PREPARATION

STEP 1   *PREPARE YOURSELF.*

STEP 2   *PREPARE YOUR AUDIENCE.*

STEP 3   *PREPARE THE SPACE.*

B. DIALOGUE

STEP 4   *USE STRATEGIC LISTENING.*

STEP 5   *USE STRATEGIC STORYTELLING.*

STEP 6   *REPEAT TO BREAK DOWN BARRIERS.*

C. NEXT STEPS

STEP 7   *MAKE AN ASK.*

STEP 8   *REFLECT AND EVALUATE.*

STEP 9   *REPEAT PROCESS.*

At the end of any strategic dialogue attempt, whether it went well or poorly, take some time to pause and reflect on how it all went.

What did you learn? What would you do differently next time? Did you make mistakes? Did they respond in unexpected ways? Did you accomplish things you're proud of, however small they may be?

Keep in mind, a single dialogue isn't likely to change everything. People change over time, and sometimes it can take a lot of dialogue before something noticeable shifts. (That's why there's a "repeat process" step at the end.) Of course, you might be surprised by what you can accomplish in a single dialogue—or you might get absolutely nowhere and decide that your "repeat" will be with someone new.

Every person is different, and no two dialogue attempts will go the same way. That's okay. Give yourself time to process and evaluate, and use what you learn in one attempt to help you out in the next one.

In case you find that some things didn't go according to plan, here are a few "what ifs" and some thoughts on how to respond in the future.

What If They Wouldn't Meet You for Dialogue?

Remember the LGBT-Christian college dialogue events I mentioned in Chapter 3? Most of them went remarkably well, but not all of them went according to plan. At one of the events, I was surprised to discover that almost no one had shown up from the campus Christian groups. A number of the LGBT students had shown up with their allies, but with virtually no conservative Christians in attendance, the whole event felt incredibly lopsided, forcing me to rework the evening's structure on the fly.

Afterward, I tried to figure out what had gone wrong.

I had planned this event in cooperation with the campus LGBT organization, with the understanding that they'd help promote it across the campus as an event for dialogue between the LGBT community and the Christian community. My first thought was that perhaps they'd failed to do their part in promoting the event, but that wasn't the problem; they'd put up a number of fliers. So why had only one side of the dialogue shown up?

I checked to see if the LGBT group had reached out personally to the campus Christian groups, to directly invite them to the event. They had, although they hadn't heard much back from them. I also checked to see if perhaps we'd unintentionally scheduled the event at the same time as another major event that might draw the Christian groups away. But no, we hadn't; we'd intentionally scheduled it on a night that none of the Christian groups had a meeting, and there wasn't anything else scheduled that night that should have disproportionately impacted the Christian students.

So what was going on?

Curious, I reached out to a few of the Christians on campus, and the problem immediately became clear.

Something about the advertising of this particular event—combined, perhaps, with the history of the groups on campus—had given the impression that "dialogue" was code for "come and listen while we tell you why you're wrong." Just as the LGBT students wouldn't have wanted to go to an event to hear the Christians preach at them, the Christians didn't want to go to an event to be lectured by the LGBT students. The promotion for this event didn't make clear exactly what would be going on, but since it was sponsored by the LGBT group on campus, those who didn't share that group's views simply assumed it was going to be a one-sided event and didn't bother to show up. Yes, they knew their presence was desired, but who wants to go to an event just to hear someone else tell you how wrong they think you are?

From that point forward, I worked to make sure any future events spelled out the event's purpose more clearly, and attendance improved significantly.

This is an important lesson for anyone struggling to get the other side to come to the table for a dialogue, whether it's a group event or just a one-on-one conversation. *You've got to make your intentions clear and ensure the other side understands the goals for the dialogue. Otherwise, they may not show up.*

Remember the discussion about what dialogue *is* and *isn't*? Many people have had bad experiences with "dialogue"; they assume that you're going to say that everyone's views are equally valid (which they don't believe) or that the "dialogue" you're asking for is really going to be a one-sided monologue where you talk at them but aren't really interested in listening to them. If they're going to have an interest in showing up, they need to know that they're going to have something valuable to contribute. You have to demonstrate that you're truly willing to listen to them, not just talk at them, and that their presence and ideas *matter* to you.

Even if you think you've communicated this to them, you may be surprised to learn that your invitation hasn't come across the way you intended. They may be so blinded by their own misconceptions about you that they assume negative motives for you that aren't really there. So it's worth following up to check with them to ensure they understand *both* your genuine willingness to hear from them in this dialogue *and* your willingness to accept that they may think you're wrong and that they're allowed to express that view as part of this dialogue.

If you've done all this and someone still isn't willing to have a dialogue, it may be that they just don't see any value in the dialogue. For dialogue to work, both parties have to be invested in it; both sides have to see some benefit to understanding each other,

For dialogue to work, both parties have to be invested in it.

or at least recognize that a successful dialogue can get them something that they want. If they don't see a benefit, you're not going to make much progress unless you can convince them there's something in this for them.

As we saw in Chapter 4, there are a lot of things someone might see as valuable about dialogue—an opportunity to avoid a controversy, to have their views heard, to resolve relationship tensions, to end a stalemate, or to make a case for something they believe in. Some people just naturally want to get along with or connect with people, and they may jump at a chance for dialogue just for its own sake as something they enjoy. But lots of people may see dialogue as intimidating or a waste of time, especially if they've already made up their minds about you or the views you stand for. In the midst of their busy lives, why should they make time to "dialogue" with someone they already know they disagree with?

This is where it's up to you to make a good case for why it's worth it *to them* to make the time. Don't just make a case for why *you'd* like it, unless it's someone so close to you that your happiness itself might be a motivator for them.

If you've done all that and they still won't dialogue, it may be out of your hands for now. Sometimes, due to their own stubbornness, assumptions about you, or other factors, people simply aren't in the right headspace to sit down for a conversation. Clarify your intentions for them once more and let them know the door is open, but don't put your life on hold while waiting to talk to someone who isn't interested in talking to you. Unfortunately, there's only so much you can do.

What If They Only Wanted to Argue?

This one can be really frustrating. You sit down to have a thoughtful, gracious dialogue with someone, and you're fully prepared to hold your tongue when necessary and do your part to make this conversation productive, but the other person keeps trying to goad you into an argument, no matter what you say or do.

If this happens, there are a couple of things to check for.

First, did you set any ground rules or expectations for the dialogue? If not, go back and do that. It doesn't have to be overly formal; it can be as simple as a mutual agreement to listen and try to understand each other, along with an acknowledgment that you don't agree with each other and you're not trying to gloss over that.

Second, check that you remembered to listen to them first rather than trying to make your case first. Often, when someone keeps interrupting you to share their own thoughts, it's a sign that they don't feel they've been fully heard yet. Even if you've already heard them some, try stopping and giving them a chance to finish saying everything they wanted to say, and check to see if they feel as though you've done a good job hearing them out and actually understanding their point of view. If not, that's where you still need to do some work.

If you've set ground rules and they agree that you've fully listened to them, but they still can't seem to keep themselves from interrupting you, it may be worth gently reminding them of the ground rules you agreed to. Be careful here, though; this can easily come across as a condescending lecture on your part, which will only increase the tension and make the whole dialogue much harder. The subtler you can be, the better.

Sometimes, though, even when you've done everything right,

you'll find that someone just keeps trying to argue with you and doesn't seem to have any intention of listening.

I was recently in a dialogue that went like that. My friend Greg, who is gay, had been dealing with a lot of hurtful, unkind remarks from his friend Sam, who is straight and a conservative Christian. Greg knows that I have a lot of these kinds of conversations, so he asked for my advice. I offered to be a kind of mediator in the conversation, and I contacted Sam to see if he'd be willing to talk to me. He said he was.

In this case, I wasn't trying to convince Sam to change his beliefs about the morality of homosexuality. I only wanted to help him understand what Greg was going through, to help the two of them get to a point where they could still have some kind of friendship even though they disagreed on this important religious question.

From the beginning, though, there were problems. Sam refused to talk face-to-face or by phone; he only wanted to exchange messages online. When I asked about his views, he offered only short answers. And as the conversation continued, we could barely get a few sentences to each other without his hurling a series of insults at me.

Eventually, it became clear that Sam just wasn't invested in this dialogue.

I had expected that the possibility of restoring his relationship with Greg would be enough to get Sam invested. But in hindsight, it's clear that Sam didn't see this dialogue as a way to get anything he wanted. Perhaps he didn't have faith that a dialogue with me would help him restore his relationship with Greg. Perhaps he had already made up his mind that he didn't want a relationship with Greg until Greg's mind changed. Whatever the case, he was eager to debate, but he wasn't interested in dialogue.

Of all the possible motivations for people to agree to dialogue, I've learned the hard way that there's one motivation to watch for: You'll find that some people are willing to dialogue only because they enjoy *debating*; their sole motivation to talk to you is so they can *win the argument*. This is a red flag. For the dialogue to be successful, they have to be at least somewhat willing to *listen* as well as talk. It's okay if someone wants to convince you that they're right; most people want that. But there needs to be at least something of value for them in the dialogue besides winning for the sake of winning: They need to have some kind of personal investment in seeing this thing through. If someone wants to dialogue because they really want you to hear them out so they can convince you to rethink your position, that's fine. But if someone wants to dialogue only because they enjoy the debate the way some people enjoy the hunt, and they have no real investment in whether you listen as long as they feel as though they won, that's not a good start for your dialogue. At that point, you either need to find something they would value that this dialogue can get them, or you need to find a new dialogue partner.

What If You Don't Feel as Though You Made Any Progress?

There is no strategy, no magic formula, that can give you unlimited power to change what people think, say, or do. And that's a good thing; if you did have that power, you'd be a comic book supervillain.

But that doesn't make it sting any less when you work hard at strategic dialogue only to find in the end that the other person doesn't budge.

It happens. And when it happens, that doesn't necessarily mean you did anything wrong.

So first, remember that change usually comes in baby steps. When you're watching for someone to go from A to Z, and they don't make it to Z, you can feel as though you've failed. But don't overlook the fact that they have made it from A to B or maybe even to C—and even that may take many rounds of dialogue. That's still a victory, even if it's not where you'd like for them to end up.

If you feel as though someone hasn't budged at all, stop and ask yourself: Is it possible that they've increased their understanding on even one point, or that they're at least slightly less opposed to your view than they were at the start? If so, hey, that's a step in the right direction. Celebrate it for what it is and remember: One step can lead to another.

Even if you don't see any immediate change right now, remember that attitude change takes time. You've planted a seed that may well bear fruit down the road, once the person is alone and has had time to think about what you've said.

I was recently contacted by someone who had known me almost fifteen years ago. All those years ago, we had had some conversations that I barely remember at all, but he still remembered them. He told me that even though he'd disagreed with me at the time, something I'd said had stuck with him. The more he thought about it, the more he was forced to rethink some long-held assumptions he'd had. In the end, he said I'd changed his mind, though by the time he was ready to admit that, we'd lost touch. You never know what impact your words may have, maybe even long after the conversation has ended.

Often, though, when a dialogue doesn't go well, there may be lessons you can learn for the future. Did you find yourself running into one or more of the five barriers? If so, which one(s)? Did you let your emotions get the best of you or find it difficult to tell the story with the other side as the protagonist? Perhaps you need to spend some more time listening and reflecting—or give yourself time away from the conversation to cool down before returning.

On the other hand, perhaps your dialogue technique was stellar but your actual arguments just weren't that strong. Maybe you need to make a better case for your position. Remember, the goal of strategic dialogue is to allow your position to be heard on its own merits; if you don't actually have good support for your position, no amount of dialogue technique will automatically win people over.

And don't forget, in the midst of all your efforts to change the other side's perspective, you may have gotten some things wrong, too. You may have had misconceptions about them or about the facts that you need to recognize in order to move forward. Your views may shift in the process of the dialogue, and that's okay. Maybe you're not wrong and you really did have everything right before you entered the dialogue, but if you find that you weren't 100 percent right in your arguments beforehand, don't let your own arrogance get in the way of acknowledging that you might have gotten some things wrong. If you did, be willing to apologize and adjust your perspective. It will make it easier for the other side to do the same when they get things wrong.

What If You've Found Success and Want to Reach a Larger Audience?

One-on-one dialogue is far more powerful than you think. The people you impact can impact others, who in turn can impact others. Don't underestimate the power of dialogue with even one person—you never know what kind of impact they'll have on the world. (You can even teach others strategic-dialogue principles to help them be more effective.)

But you may still find occasions where you'd like to reach a larger audience with your message as a speaker, blogger, community leader, etc. If so, simply adapt the underlying principles of strategic dialogue for your situation. For example, to practice *strategic listening* with a national audience, you can't literally "listen" to every member of the audience at once, but you could meet with diverse representatives of your target audience, read the writings of influential leaders, conduct surveys with open-ended questions, and so on. The essential principles are the same, and you're still trying to learn the same things; just adapt the method to make it work for you.

Even if you're in a position of national or international influence, though, don't give up on those one-on-one conversations. Not only can you impact others most deeply that way, you can also learn a lot from those conversations that you can then use to shape your public messaging.

What If They Read This Book?

One of my friends, knowing I'd been working on this book, asked me, "Are you sure you want to write a book that explains how you get people to change their minds? How do you know someone on the other side won't use it to try to counter your work?"

But the beauty of this approach to strategic dialogue is that it's not about pulling the wool over people's eyes in some way, tricking them into believing what you want. It's about clearing away the obstacles that too often get in the way of both sides' best arguments being heard and the truth coming out.

This book is written with the assumption that the other side isn't familiar with strategic dialogue, because you can't very well require someone to sit down and read a whole book about dialogue before you're even willing to have a conversation with them. Most of the time, we're entering dialogues with people who are suspicious and skeptical of us, and it's on us to do all the heavy lifting and make the conversation as smooth as possible for both sides.

But if both sides have these tools and are committed to this kind of dialogue, that's good news for everyone! It's a good thing for both sides to be working to clear away the barriers: We *shouldn't* be making decisions based on team loyalty or misconceptions or protecting our own egos. We *should* be listening to each other, telling our stories, and trying to understand one another's underlying interests. What makes these techniques so powerful is that they're honest and they're all about getting to the truth, whatever that truth may be.

So hey, if they read this book, that's great. Maybe they'll be as willing to dialogue as you are. I'd count that as a good thing.

CHAPTER 16

Hope for the Future

Can we overcome apathy? Yes, but only if we have hope.

—Jane Goodall[50]

In our modern, polarized world, with people fighting all around us and daily news stories of raging culture wars, a push for nuanced dialogue can seem like a naive fantasy. It's easy to get discouraged just sitting on the sidelines, and it's even easier to get discouraged when you try to make a difference and find yourself caught in the cross fire.

I know the challenge well. For twenty years now, I've been having regular conversations with people who think I'm wrong. I often find myself in rooms full of people who disagree with me, where I have to sit quietly and listen while people say things that frustrate or upset me. I read books written by people whose views I vehemently disagree with; sometimes I even find myself mentioned in their books, and I get to read about what a villain they think I am because they disagree with a position I've taken. Even when I'm not directly seeking out these conversations, I still find myself in all kinds of situations where people ask what I do for a living; I tell them, and they're quick to let me know in no uncertain terms just how much they disagree with me and what I stand for.

Maybe you're like me, in a situation where your daily life revolves in one way or another around an issue of importance to you. Or maybe it's something that comes up only once in a while. Either way, you're likely to find times when you're frankly just tired of having this conversation. What do you do then?

"I don't know how you do it," a friend of mine recently said. "I can't stay in a room with some of these people for five minutes before my blood starts boiling. How do you keep from getting upset?"

The truth is, I *do* get upset. When you care deeply about an issue, of *course* it's upsetting to hear people attack your point of view or promote a view that you believe is harmful. It's upsetting, and it's exhausting. You'd have to be superhuman not to be affected by it.

Over the years, I've learned some techniques to help me stay publicly calm even when I'm crying or fuming inside. For instance, I try to keep a pad of paper with me in stressful situations so I can write down my upset thoughts instead of voicing them in the moment; it's much better to be taking notes while someone else talks than to be angrily interrupting them, and it gives me the opportunity to consider my words and address the issues later when I'm not so upset. I pray before (and during) difficult conversations. I remind myself over and over again that the people on the other side of the table from me are operating from a different set of assumptions and that I might make the same mistakes I believe they're making if I were in their shoes with their beliefs and experiences. When a conversation gets too tense, I often try to steer things back to points of commonality.

But I've also learned how important it is to know my own limits and be willing to step away from a conversation before it becomes too much. Sometimes I simply have to say to someone, "I think I need to take a break from this conversation for now; I feel myself getting very emotional, and I don't want to say anything that would damage our friendship." I've never yet been sorry I said those words. I've been sorry only when I didn't say them soon enough. (And yes, there are many times I didn't step away when I should have, and I regret every one of those times.)

The same thing is true for larger cultural conversations: Sometimes I have to turn off the television, put down the book, or step out of the conference room because I realize I've heard as much as I can take in that moment. It's important to be exposed to what the other side is saying, but it's also important to know when I need a breather to pray or think or call a friend for encouragement.

None of us are superhuman. Don't forget to take care of yourself.

On the television show *CSI*, crime scene investigator Gil Grissom spends his workday dealing with death and horror—so to unwind, he rides roller coasters. At first, that sounds out of character for someone in such a serious role, but I think it makes perfect sense. Personally, I like to invite friends over for board game nights so we can talk and laugh and temporarily focus on something of no real-world consequence whatsoever. Other times, I go into a room by myself, lock the door, and listen to music until I've vented as much emotion as I can. Some people deal with their stress by watching dumb sitcoms or playing video games or relaxing in a bubble bath with classical music on. As a Christian, I also like to pray. A lot.

Find your own healthy way to unwind, whether it's an exercise routine, a regular movie night, or quiet time with a good book. Find what helps you get away from the stress of real life and stick to it. Strategic dialogue can be emotionally draining, and it's important to build yourself back up so you don't burn out.

You Will Make Mistakes

Even with all my experience in this work, I still make mistakes all the time. I know how important it is not to let dialogues turn into arguments, but I still sometimes let my temper get the best of me. I interrupt people even when I shouldn't, and I take things personally although I know better. But with all my mistakes, I've still seen a lot of people change their minds as a result of our dialogues. It's possible to be effective even when you're nowhere near perfect. (Isn't that a relief?)

If you decide to take on this kind of dialogue work, you're going to make mistakes. You'll realize too late that you said the wrong thing or that you gave in to your emotions when you should have stayed calm. Learn from these experiences, but don't beat yourself up over them. You're human. You're fallible. There's always room for you to improve.

There are two important things to remember here. The first is that any attempt at dialogue is better than no attempt at dialogue. You won't always say the right thing, but just making the effort to reach across the divide is a powerful thing by itself. Imagine if everyone in the world made that kind of effort every day! It would completely transform the world we live in. So don't stop. If you fail, get back up and try again. Practice listening. Practice building bridges. You'll never be perfect, but with practice, you will get better, and every time you reach out, you make a positive impact in the world.

Any attempt at dialogue is better than no attempt at dialogue.

At the same time, the second thing to remember is that this isn't all on you. You're one person, and while you are capable of making a tremendous impact, you can't carry the entire weight of your chosen issue(s) on your shoulders alone. Some people won't be willing to listen to you even when you do everything perfectly. Others may have their mind changed by even your most flawed attempt to dialogue with them. At the end of the day, you can only do what you can do, so don't allow yourself to slip into believing that the fate of the entire world is all on you. That kind of pressure can discourage and paralyze you, and it's simply not realistic. Wherever possible, share the load, talk about your successes and failures with others who support you, and when all is said and done, remember that it's not all about you.

Final Thoughts

We live in a polarized world, surrounded by polarized thinking.

The truth is, dialogue is powerful, but it's not always fun. It takes a lot of discipline, and not everyone is willing to dedicate the time and energy that it takes.

This kind of work isn't easy. Dialogue is hard. Bridge-building is hard. Diplomacy is hard.

Sometimes it means listening attentively while someone spouts ideas that you know are wrong and damaging. Sometimes it means standing in the middle of a conflict and getting hate thrown at you from both sides.

It can wear you out. It can make you sad. It can make you angry.

It's far easier to just talk to the people who agree with you and post snarky comments about the other folks on social media. Some days that's all you'll feel like doing, especially when dialogue hasn't moved things as quickly as you wish it would.

But when you find yourself wanting to quit, convinced that nothing you do is making a bit of difference, don't give up. Keep going. You won't see immediate results every time, and sometimes, you won't see any results at all. Keep doing it anyway.

We need people out there taking a stand for grace and dialogue. We need people who won't give in to our culture's penchant for polarization.

Because that polarization is killing us. And the only way out of it is for people like you to do the difficult, thankless, exhausting work of sitting down to talk to your opponents, to listen to them, to try to understand how they see the world and why they do what they do, and to become a voice they will listen to, helping them understand new perspectives and helping them change their attitudes without fear that everything else will come tumbling down around them if they do.

You have that power. And there may be some people for whom you *alone* have that influence. They might listen to you even if they won't listen to anyone else who shares your views.

Maybe, when all is said and done, Aunt Gertrude and Uncle John don't change their minds. Still, don't stop. There are people out there who need to see your patience and your persistence in the face of that opposition. Gain a reputation as a bridge-builder in all aspects of your life. Be the person everyone knows they can come to with their views and their questions and who they know won't treat them as an enemy. And inspire others to do the same.

Our society has a choice to make in this age of always-on, ever-expanding connections. We can choose to build our own communities, drawing lines to say who's in and who's out, surrounding ourselves with people who will reinforce us in our belief that we are so much better than the people out there are. Or we can choose to do the difficult work of reaching across those lines, using this incredible technology of connection to learn about the people we think we have nothing in common with, letting them be the protagonists of their own stories as we find ways to join them in those stories and build a better world together for all of us.

One of those ways is easy, and it leads to a fractured and fractious society where we are constantly fighting for power and no one can agree on the truth. The other way is hard, but it can lead us to new discoveries and opportunities we've never had before in all of human history.

The next step starts with you.

ACKNOWLEDGMENTS

This book has been shaped by the influences of more people than I could possibly name, but there are a few I must single out for extra appreciation.

First, this book would not be what it is without the invaluable input of my editor, Lauren Appleton, who championed this project while whipping the manuscript into shape.

Many thanks to my agent, Greg Daniel, who has not only helped me find the right publishers for my books but who has also helped at every stage of the process to make them the best they could be. This book would not exist without his support.

This book also wouldn't exist without the insight of Martin Camper, who selflessly worked with me on the concept and structure and who encouraged me to pursue this when I hesitated. My conversations with Martin echo throughout the pages of this book in ways he may never fully know.

Christopher Broskie deserves so much credit for the many hours he spent helping me refine and streamline this book to be as accessible as possible, telling me honestly when things just weren't working and helping me get them working again.

The idea of talking "across the divide" has been strongly influenced by the work of Maggie Heineman and the members of the 1990s organization Bridges Across the Divide. I am so grateful to them for starting me down this path and showing me what productive cross-divide dialogue looks like in practice. I am particularly grateful to Sonia Balcer for her friendship across our own divide and for demonstrating repeatedly what it means to treat your cultural opponents with compassion. To this day, I ask myself, "What would Sonia do?" in difficult situations.

I am deeply indebted to Beth Zemsky for introducing me to key concepts in cross-cultural dialogue research that are covered in this book. Thanks are also due to Mark Pezzo, who first introduced me to some of the social psychology work that has shaped my approach.

There are a number of people who deserve personal thanks for their support of me and of this project in a variety of ways. Among them, I especially need to thank Linda Robertson, Matt Carden, Matthew Vines, Rachel Held Evans, Ralph Blair, Ron Belgau, Wendy Grisham, Wendy Gritter, and Wesley Hill. Each of you has made an incredible impact on me and helped make this book possible. Your friendship and wisdom mean the world to me.

Thank you to everyone who supported my nonprofit work over the years and enabled me to have the many conversations across the divide that informed this book. I am forever in your debt.

To Kathryn Andriotis, Jonathan Lee, Elizabeth and Ben

Steere, and Ann Tillery, thank you all for your love and encouragement.

To Asad, Earl, Gonzalo, Ian, Matt, Matthew, Seth, and Ty, a special thanks for keeping me sane through some difficult times.

To my dad, thank you for your love and support and for all the lessons you taught me that made their way into this book.

And finally, there's a reason my late mom gets several mentions in this book. Out of all the people I've ever known in my life, she was perhaps the most gifted at empathy and getting people who disagreed to work together for a common purpose. The world needs more people like her, and my goal is to live up to her example. I love you, Mom. We miss you.

NOTES

1   First inaugural address of Abraham Lincoln, March 4, 1861,
    http://avalon.law.yale.edu/19th_century/lincoln1.asp.

2   "The Partisan Divide on Political Values Grows Even Wider,"
    Pew Research Center, October 5, 2017, http://www.people
    -press.org/2017/10/05/the-partisan-divide-on-political-values
    -grows-even-wider.

3   "The Partisan Divide on Political Values Grows Even Wider:
    Partisan Animosity, Personal Politics, Views of Trump," Pew
    Research Center, October 5, 2017, http://www.people-press
    .org/2017/10/05/8-partisan-animosity-personal-politics-views
    -of-trump.

4   "The Partisan Divide on Political Values Grows Even Wider:
    Partisan Animosity, Personal Politics, Views of Trump"; also
    Kiley, Jocelyn. "In Polarized Era, Fewer Americans Hold a
    Mix of Conservative and Liberal Views," Pew Research
    Center, October 23, 2017, http://www.pewresearch.org/fact

-tank/2017/10/23/in-polarized-era-fewer-americans-hold-a
-mix-of-conservative-and-liberal-views.

5   Pariser, Eli. *The Filter Bubble: What the Internet Is Hiding from You.*
New York: The Penguin Press, 2011.

6   Pariser, *The Filter Bubble*, 2.

7   Constine, Josh. "Facebook Now Has 2 Billion Monthly
Users . . . and Responsibility." TechCrunch, June 27, 2017,
https://techcrunch.com/2017/06/27/facebook-2-billion-users.

8   "Blue Feed, Red Feed." *Wall Street Journal*, graphics.wsj.com
/blue-feed-red-feed.

9   North, Ryan. *Dinosaur Comics*, September 13, 2017, http://www
.qwantz.com/?comic=3187.

10 "The Bubble," on *Saturday Night Live*, season 42, episode 7,
"Kristen Wiig/The XX," NBC, November 19, 2016.

11 Asch, S. E. "Effects of Group Pressure upon the Modification
and Distortion of Judgment." In *Groups, Leadership and Men*, ed.
H. Guetzkow, 177–90. Pittsburgh: Carnegie Press, 1951.

12 Lamm, Helmut, and David G. Myers. "Group-Induced
Polarization of Attitudes and Behavior." *Advances in
Experimental Social Psychology* 11 (1978): 145–95.

13 Harrison, Emma. "Mrs. Roosevelt Explains a Tea." *New York Times*, October 15, 1960.

14 Twain, Mark. Speech quoted in Society of the Army of the Tennessee, *Report of the Proceedings of the Society of the Army of the Tennessee at the Thirteenth Annual Meeting Held at Chicago, Illinois, November 12th and 13th, 1879*, 354.

15 Hemingway, Ernest. "Monologue to the Maestro: A High Seas Letter." *Esquire*, October 1935, 174B.

16 Schwartz, Stephen, and Gregory Maguire. 2004. *Wicked: A New Musical.*

17 Fisher, Roger, William Ury, and Bruce Patton. *Getting to Yes: Negotiating Agreement Without Giving In*. 3rd ed. New York: Penguin Books, 2011.

18 Carnegie, Dale. *How to Win Friends & Influence People*. New York: Pocket Books, 1998. First published 1936 by Simon & Schuster.

19 Chu, Jeff. *Does Jesus Really Love Me?: A Gay Christian's Pilgrimage in Search of God in America*. New York: Harper, 2013.

20 Bawer, Bruce. *A Place at the Table: The Gay Individual in American Society*. New York: Touchstone, 1993, 44.

21 Cohen, Geoffrey L. "Party Over Policy: The Dominating Impact of Group Influence on Political Beliefs." *Journal of Personality and Social Psychology* 85, no. 5 (November 2003): 808–22.

22 Cohen, "Party Over Policy," 819.

23 *The Eye of the Storm.* Directed by William Peters. New York: ABC, 1970.

24 Sherif, Muzafer, et al. *Intergroup Conflict and Cooperation: The Robbers Cave Experiment.* Norman, OK: University Book Exchange, 1961.

25 Hastorf, Albert H., and Hadley Cantril. "They Saw a Game: A Case Study." *Journal of Abnormal and Social Psychology* 49, no. 1 (January 1954): 129–34.

26 Munroe, Randall. "Duty Calls." *xkcd*, http://www.xkcd.com /386.

27 Angelou, Maya. *Singin' and Swingin' and Gettin' Merry Like Christmas.* New York: Random House, 1976.

28 Bennett, Milton. "A Developmental Approach to Training for Intercultural Sensitivity." *International Journal of Intercultural Relations* 10, no. 2 (December 1986): 179–96.

29 Lee, Justin. *Torn: Rescuing the Gospel from the Gays-vs.-Christians Debate*. New York: Jericho Books, 2012, 77–81.

30 *The Simpsons*, season 1, episode 9, "Life on the Fast Lane," Fox, March 18, 1990.

31 Le Guin, Ursula K. "Prophets and Mirrors: Science Fiction as a Way of Seeing," *The Living Light* 7, no. 3 (Fall 1970). In *The Language of the Night: Essays on Fantasy and Science Fiction*, ed. Susan Wood, 31. New York: Putnam, 1989.

32 DeGeneres, Ellen. *Ellen DeGeneres: Here and Now*. HBO, June 25, 2003.

33 John 18:38.

34 Munroe, Randall. "Ten Thousand." *xkcd*, http://www.xkcd .com/1053.

35 Bacon, Francis. *The New Organon*, XLVI, 1620.

36 "Why Doesn't America Read Anymore?" NPR, April 1, 2014, https://www.npr.org/2014/04/01/297690717/why-doesnt -america-read-anymore.

37 Hays, Brooks. "Scientists Say Sniffing Farts Could Prevent Cancer." United Press International, July 11, 2014, https://

www.upi.com/Science_News/2014/07/11/385140510
2633.

38 Sloman, Steven, and Philip Fernbach. *The Knowledge Illusion: Why We Never Think Alone.* New York: Riverhead, 2017.

39 Rozenblit, Leonid, and Frank Keil. "The Misunderstood Limits of Folk Science: An Illusion of Explanatory Depth." *Cognitive Science* 26 (2002): 521–62.

40 Sloman and Fernbach, *The Knowledge Illusion*, 192.

41 Lord, Charles G., Lee Ross, and Mark R. Lepper. "Biased Assimilation and Attitude Polarization: The Effects of Prior Theories on Subsequently Considered Evidence." *Journal of Personality and Social Psychology* 37, no. 11 (1979): 2098–109.

42 Lord, Ross, and Lepper, "Biased Assimilation and Attitude Polarization," 2098.

43 Ross, Lee, Mark R. Lepper, and Michael Hubbard. "Perseverance in Self-Perception and Social Perception: Biased Attributional Processes in the Debriefing Paradigm." *Journal of Personality and Social Psychology* 32, no. 5 (1975): 880–92.

44 King, Martin Luther, Jr. *Strength to Love.* Minneapolis, MN: Fortress Press, 2010. First published 1963 by Harper & Row.

45 "Can Likely Voter Models Be Improved?," Pew Research
Center, January 7, 2016, http://www.pewresearch.org/2016
/01/07/measuring-the-likelihood-to-vote.

46 McGonigal, Jane. "Gaming Can Make a Better World."
Recorded February 2010 at TED2010. TED video, 19:57,
https://www.ted.com/talks/jane_mcgonigal_gaming_can
_make_a_better_world.

47 Mercier, Hugo, and Dan Sperber. *The Enigma of Reason.*
Cambridge, MA: Harvard University Press, 2017, 226.

48 *Better Off Ted*, season 1, episode 10, "Trust and Consequence,"
ABC, July 14, 2009.

49 Lee, Harper. *To Kill a Mockingbird.* New York: Harper
Perennial, 2002, 128. First published 1960 by J. B. Lippincott
Company.

50 Goodall, Jane. "The Power of One." *Time*, August 26, 2002,
87.

Justin Lee is a writer and activist who has spent more than twenty years bridging cultural divides.

He is the founder and former executive director of the world's largest LGBT Christian advocacy organization, where he was known for working across political, social, and theological lines to bring people together. His first book, *Torn: Rescuing the Gospel from the Gays-vs.-Christians Debate*, has been widely cited for its role in helping conservative Christian parents accept their LGBT kids.

Justin has spoken around the world on overcoming polarization and continues to be popular with both conservative and liberal audiences. He currently serves as the executive director of Nuance Ministries. He lives in Orlando, Florida.

Join the conversation! Justin invites ongoing dialogue at **GeekyJustin.com.**